Merry Christmas

my Love!

Adele

Tree-Ring Management

Take the Long View and Grow Your Business Slowly

Tree-Ring Management

Take the Long View and Grow Your Business Slowly

HIROSHI TSUKAKOSHI

塚
越
寛

Translated by
Hart Larrabee

Japan Publishing Industry Foundation for Culture

Published by Japan Publishing Industry Foundation for Culture (JPIC)
3-12-3 Kanda-Jinbocho, Chiyoda-ku, Tokyo 101-0051, Japan

Tree-Ring Management: Take the Long View and Grow Your Business Slowly
Risutora Nashino 'Nenrin Keiei' : Ii Kaisha Wa 'Tooki Wo Hakari' Yukkuri Seicho

Originally published in Japanese by Kobunsha Co., Ltd.
in 2009 and 2014
English publishing rights arranged with Kobunsha Co., Ltd.

Japanese editing: Hirofumi Kabashima
Jacket and cover design: Hisanori Niizuma [gift inc.]
Front and cover photo: © Mitsushi Okada/orion /amanaimages

As this book is published primarily to be donated to public libraries,
educational institutions, etc., commercial publication rights are available.
For all enquiries regarding these rights, please contact the publisher at the
following address: japanlibrary@jpic.or.jp

http://www.jpic.or.jp/japanlibrary/

ISBN 978-4-916055-46-0

On the Publication of the English Edition

This book is an English translation of *Risutora nashino nenrin keiei* (Tree-Ring Management with No Downsizing), originally published by Kobunsha in 2009 and revised in 2014.

To my pleasant surprise, many people in Japan have picked up the book since then, and it has also been featured on television and in other media. It seems people have been particularly drawn to it by our company's 48 consecutive years of rising sales and rising profits.

But I would ask those who take this book in hand to stop and think for a moment: Are rising sales and rising profits really all that important? I don't think so. The important thing is the happiness of employees and everyone else who is involved with the company. One of the things I am most proud of at my company is that for the last 20 years, no one has left the company because they were unhappy. Isn't this of greater value than rising sales and rising profits?

Except perhaps for the sort of elites who carry the weight of a nation on their shoulders, stability is what brings people happiness, leading stable, secure lives. Everyone wants a happy home, even if it is a modest one.

I believe this is a point that companies must better understand: a company should be a place where managers strive to safeguard the livelihoods of their employees. I do not believe that growth is more important than this.

There are reports in the news every day about corporate personnel cuts and manpower shortages, but our company, which has stuck to tree-ring management that aims for slow growth just as a tree adds rings, has never faced either problem. Our employees all seem happy and secure in their work, and their smiles bring me great joy.

I am a bit anxious about how useful my management theories will prove when studied overseas, but I must leave this to the judgment of my readers. I hope this book will be of help in your business and in your life.

Hiroshi Tsukakoshi, Chairman
Ina Food Industry Co., Ltd.
January 2015

Introduction

The financial crisis in the United States, precipitated by subprime lending, ushered in a worldwide economic downturn. In Japan, too, many companies saw a decline in performance as the winds of recession raged, just as they had after the collapse of the "bubble economy" in the early 1990s.

The failure of the major American securities firm Lehman Brothers in 2008 left me feeling indignant. Until shortly before then, its management had been drawing salaries tallied in the millions of dollars, yet the company's sudden bankruptcy left its employees, trading partners, and indeed, the whole world in a terrible mess.

I have little patience for the sort of people who fool around with numbers for a living, yet there now seem to be far too many managers and far too many companies that have lost sight of the way things really ought to be. When it comes to management, "the way things really ought to be" means building the kind of company that contributes to society by making its employees happy. Sales and profits are nothing more than a means of achieving this end.

This might be easier to understand if you think of a

company as a family. When a family runs short of food, it does not expel one of its members so these who remain can eat what is left. A company is the same. Just as you wish for the happiness of your family, it is important to wish for the happiness of your employees; doing so generates a succession of virtuous cycles in company management. This is the secret to Ina Food Industry's continually rising revenues and profits over the course of half a century.

Ninety-nine percent of the companies in Japan are small and medium-sized enterprises (SMEs) with fewer than 300 employees. Such companies account for 69% of Japan's workforce. Television and print media focus almost exclusively on major corporations, but it is SMEs that actually sustain Japan's economy.

I wrote this book in the hope that it will help those SMEs that now struggle against a doctrine that puts sales and profits above all else. In these hard times, I am confident that returning to the way a company really ought to be will open up new ways of doing business that enable companies to endure.

I will be very pleased if this book is even of some small use to readers.

Hiroshi Tsukakoshi

Contents

CHAPTER 2
Creating a Company That Makes Employees Happy 55

CHAPTER 3
Start With the Little Things You Can Do 105

社　是

いい会社を
つくりましょう

― たくましく そして やさしく ―

伊那食品工業株式会社

Mission Statement

Let's build a good company
—one that is strong and
compassionate.

Ina Food Industry Co., Ltd.

Timeline

1958   Ina Food Industry Co., Ltd. is established

1973   Using in-house technology, the company builds the industry's first wastewater treatment equipment

1980   Launches the Kanten Papa series of products for home use

1987   Breaks ground on Kanten Papa Gardens

1995   In recognition of his services in promoting science and technology through kanten production, President Tsukakoshi is awarded the Director-General's Prize from the Japan Science and Technology Agency

1996   For the same contributions, President Tsukakoshi is awarded the Government of Japan's Medal of Honor with Yellow Ribbon. He also receives the Minister's Prize from the Japanese Ministry of Agriculture, Forestry, and Fisheries in recognition of his services in promoting the recycling of kanten dregs

2002   Kanten Papa Hall, a multi-purpose cultural facility, opens in Kanten Papa Gardens

2006   The Papa Nanoen agricultural corporation is established. In recognition of 48 consecutive years of rising sales and rising profits, Ina Food Industry Co., Ltd. is awarded the Small and Medium Enterprise Agency's highest award, the Good Company Award

2007   For his contribution to the Indonesian seaweed industry, Chairman Tsukakoshi receives an award for meritorious service from the Indonesian government

2008   50th anniversary of the company's founding. Chairman Tsukakoshi is awarded the Environmental Management Pearl, the Japan Environmental Management Award Grand Prize

2011   Chairman Tsukakoshi receives the Order of the Rising Sun, Gold Rays with Rosette, from the Government of Japan

All currency figures originally in Japanese yen have been converted to US dollar amounts at then-prevailing rates.

CHAPTER 1

Aspire to Tree Ring Management and Your Company Will Endure

A Company Exists to Make Its Employees Happy

Ina Food Industry is a company that produces agar, a gelling agent known as *kanten* in Japanese. In addition to wholesaling kanten ingredients to food and pharmaceutical manufacturers, we also produce products for household use under the Kanten Papa brand, which may be familiar to some Japanese readers.

Ina Food Industry was founded in Nagano Prefecture's Ina Valley in 1958. Hemmed in by mountains to the east and west and bisected by the flow of the Tenryu River, the Ina Valley experiences great fluctuations in winter temperature. For a long time, farmers in the area have taken advantage of this climate to produce kanten during the winter months.

I joined Ina Food Industry six months after it was established, bringing with me the peculiar title of Acting President. I was 21 years old. At the time, the company only had a dozen or so employees, and the factory had little in the way of production equipment, no more than four motorized machines.

Losses had piled up during the company's first six months, and the company was in crisis. Ina Food Industry was a subsidiary of the lumber company where I worked, and I was sent in to engineer a turnaround. So began my desperate struggle as an inexperienced,

21-year-old Acting President.

What surprised me when I joined the company was that despite being engaged in the production of powdered kanten—something still very unusual in those days—the company had only the most rudimentary technology. I pored through books on chemistry and came up with ways to improve our production machinery.

At the same time, I was putting the accounts in order and drumming up business. I worked through weekends and holidays; my only time off was a day or two for New Year's.

Still, I was happy just to be able to work, because I had gone through a bitter experience in the past. Dreaming of attending university, I had started classes at the local prefectural school, Ina Kita High, but then come down with tuberculosis during my second year.

Forced to convalesce for the next three years, I dropped out of school and spent my days resting in a hospital room. Looking out the window, I watched people strolling in the sun, envious of how lucky they were to be able to walk.

When my illness finally subsided and I was able to work, I took a job at the lumber company. A year and a half later, I transferred to Ina Food Industry on the orders of the lumber company's president.

Today, we have more than 480 employees, and annual sales reached 17.6 billion yen (US $173 million) in fiscal year 2013. We are the leading producer of kanten in the world, and in 2006, we won the Small and Medium Enterprise Agency's highest award, the Good Company Award.

But I have not managed the company out of a desire to make the company bigger, or to increase sales, or to receive recognition. The growth of the company, its increased sales, and the various awards it has received are nothing more than consequences of our management principles. That might sound terribly self-important to some readers, but I really mean it.

My sole focus in managing the company has been to ensure that it endures, because I believe a company's greatest virtue is endurance. To be perfectly honest, for the first 20 years, I had no spare time to think about such things. I was simply desperate to survive and keep the company going.

I think it was about 25 years after joining the company, when the pressure finally began to ease a bit, that I started thinking about why companies exist and what corporate growth really means. The conclusion I reached after pondering such questions for years is that a good company exists to make its employees happy, thereby contributing to its local community and society at large.

I realized that endurance was the most important part of making this happen, because if the company fails to endure, the happiness of its employees will come to an abrupt end.

Seek Not to Be a Successful Company, But a Good Company

Having decided that a company exists to make its employees happy and that a company's greatest virtue is endurance, I began to entertain doubts about the conventional wisdom of what defines successful management. Doctrines emphasizing sales above all, the expansion of profits, or market capitalization seem all too often to come at the expense of employee happiness.

It is impossible to manage a company whose sales do not grow, and in the absence of profits, a company's very survival may be in doubt. Yet, once you make increased sales and profits your sole objective, employee happiness becomes secondary. In short, you start to think about how profits could be effectively raised by reducing labor costs and welfare expenditures, or by cutting back on activities that give back to the community and support culture and the arts.

This seems completely backward to me. Management

is all about finding a balance between the company's numbers and the happiness of its employees. This balance is what management should pursue above all else. Corporate management these days seems to have placed too much emphasis on company numbers, throwing things out of balance.

The mission statement of Ina Food Industry is, "Let's build a good company—one that is strong and compassionate." I always tell my employees that we should seek to build not a successful company, but a good company. Talking about a "successful company" always seems to carry the impression that numbers are the priority, that sales or profits are growing rapidly, that the stock price is rising, or that salaries are high. To be sure, the conventional view would suggest that such a company is truly successful.

But it would give me no joy if Ina Food Industry were called a successful company by these standards. Instead, I hope that we will be called a "good company." Being a good company means more than just having good operational numbers; it means being the sort of company that will be called a good company in everyday conversation. I strive to ensure that not just our employees, but also our suppliers, clients, consumers, and community will speak about us in this way.

As you can probably guess, a company that tries to increase its own profits by putting unreasonable pressure on its trading partners is not one that will be called a good company. And a good company certainly does not engage in business practices that deceive consumers, like mislabeling food products. A company whose employees work under stressful, unpleasant conditions is not a good one, no matter how generous its salaries may be— and that isn't what employees want, anyway. A company that does not give back to its community is unlikely to be considered a good company by those who live nearby.

We rarely use the term "successful company" in everyday conversation. Instead, we use the phrase "good company," because it more naturally expresses how we feel. And when we use it, we are not talking about the company's balance sheet, but our favorable impression of the company as a whole.

I often ask visitors to our company if they asked their taxi driver what kind of a company Ina Food Industry is. I'm pretty sure most drivers in the area would respond to the question by saying, "It's a good company." Taxi drivers may not know much about the internal workings of Ina Food Industry, or the state of its finances, or how our numbers look, but they do know that our company gives back to the community and they recognize that our employees are polite and quick to offer a pleasant smile.

A good company makes everyone involved, including those on the inside, happy. This is what it means to build a "good company."

Management Is Taking the Long View

Sontoku Ninomiya, the 19th-century agricultural leader, moralist, and economist, once wrote, "Those who take the long view will prosper. Those who are short-sighted will become poor." I came across these words perhaps 30 years ago, around the time I began to think that a company's greatest virtue is endurance. It suddenly struck me then that in order to build a good company that would endure, I needed to take the long view.

Ever since then, my management strategy has been to take the long view. It is easy enough to discuss but difficult to put into practice. Recently it has become even more difficult, because companies are now called upon to raise profits over short periods. The demands of the stock market require that listed companies settle their accounts every quarter.

The negative management implications of this are not inconsequential. In simplest terms, it takes a great deal of work to put together financial reports every quarter—an enormous amount of effort when you consider that every company in Japan is doing it. If all this labor were put to productive use, it would surely be enough to get a great deal of real work done.

But the greater problem is that being overly conscious of quarterly reports leads to the neglect of medium- and long-term initiatives. Focusing too intently on generating short-term profit makes it impossible to manage in a way that takes the long view. There is a tendency to slip into the doctrine of the supremacy of numbers and to foster a culture that says everything is all right as long as the numbers are all right.

With this mindset, you can get away with managing in a way that claims everything is good as long as the numbers are good right now. This reminds me of the failure of the major American securities firm Lehman Brothers, which went bankrupt in September 2008 with $613 billion in liabilities. Just a few years earlier, the company was generating enormous profits from subprime loans and similar investments. Executives earned more than $10 million per year, and it was not at all uncommon for employees to take home annual salaries of $300,000 or more.

And yet this massive securities firm suddenly went bankrupt. People could not believe their ears when they heard the news. It was a classic example, I believe, of chasing short-term profits and neglecting to take the long view. I can still see the television clips of employees leaving the corporate headquarters with cardboard boxes in their arms. For some reason, many of those on their way out were smiling as if to say, "Well, see you later!"

Those boxes were filled with personal belongings, but they must surely have also contained data related to the work each employee had been responsible for. Taking such data with them, of course, would help them find new employment. It was as if they felt that as long as they had such data in hand, then they did not need to care what became of the company—or so it appeared to me, at least.

I felt as if I were witnessing the endpoint of American-style capitalism and individualism. My sense is that American management methods do not make people happy. At the very least, they are incompatible with my own principles of management. I have taken the following words from Sontoku Ninomiya as the pillar of my own management strategy. Even today, they have not aged a bit.

> Those who take the long view will prosper.
> Those who are shortsighted will become poor.
> Those who take the long view

Plant cedar seedlings for a century hence,
And by sowing in spring what can be harvested in fall, they prosper.

Those who are shortsighted
Do not sow in spring what can only be harvested in the distant fall.
Lost in the imagined riches before them, they set it aside.
Failing to plant, they see only visions of reaping,
And so, grow poor.

Sontoku Ninomiya

Rapid Growth Is the Enemy – Aim for Tree-Ring Management

Through 2005, Ina Foods maintained rising income and rising profits for almost the entire 48 years since its inception in 1958. This comes as the result of developing our own markets for kanten, a decidedly low-key product, and nurturing them slowly. By continually increasing income and profits, we have been able to develop substantial equity of our own and have managed to get by with almost no debt.

People are often amazed that we have been able to

maintain rising income and rising profits for such a long time, but I think it is the natural result of trying to manage with a long-term view and wanting the company to endure. As with any company, there have been ups and downs, but I have always tried to manage naturally, aiming for low growth without overstretching, in both good times and bad.

I call this management style "tree-ring management": growing a little bit each year, slowly and reliably, in the same way that a tree adds rings. I believe that this is the ideal form of management. Tree rings vary in width with each year's weather, sometimes growing a great deal and sometimes only a little, but the tree always grows bigger than it was the year before. Even if a given ring happens to be narrow, the important thing is that the tree continues to grow.

Tree rings tend to be particularly wide in young trees, and grow narrower with the passage of years. I think the same holds true for companies. Naturally, young companies tend to grow more quickly. With the passage of years, their rate of growth slows, but as the trunk (that is, the company) grows thicker, their growth, in absolute terms, increases. Trees also do not force themselves to grow unreasonably. The parts of trees with wider rings are relatively weak, while those with narrower rings are hard and strong. I think this is also something we should learn from.

The greatest enemy of tree-ring management is rapid growth. Indeed, there is nothing a manager should fear more than rapid growth. I will have more to say about this later, but in the past, our company has received proposals from major supermarket chains to roll out our products nationwide. After thinking about it carefully, I always turned them down. Having our products in supermarkets would surely bring rapid sales growth, but I decided that growing more quickly than we anticipated could cause us to stumble later. I chose instead to grow a little bit every year, just like the rings of a tree, even if this meant growing at a slower pace.

Yet despite my commitment to tree-ring management, I found myself swept up in a surging tide that even I found difficult to resist: the kanten boom of 2005. Health programs on television started popularizing the health benefits of kanten, triggering a sudden spike in demand. We already knew that the water-soluble dietary fiber contained in kanten was good for the body, but the new publicity created a diet craze that greatly increased demand for our products.

Even so, I would normally have avoided taking the plunge with an unreasonable increase in production, but this time I found myself moved by requests from the elderly and people in the health and welfare industry who wanted to use our products and asked that they be made more widely available. I told our employees that I was not interested in rapid growth, but explained that there was a surge in demand from customers who really wanted our kanten products. I asked them what we should do and they replied, "If that's the case, then let's do it."

And so in 2005, we embarked on a round-the-clock effort to increase kanten production that was unlike anything ever before attempted at Ina Foods. As a result, sales that year went up 40% year-over-year. This unprecedented rate of growth, though, left me feeling more anxious than overjoyed.

Sure enough, the kanten boom passed and sales fell starting in 2006. Profits, too, declined year-over-year. Since we had not made any unwarranted investment in facilities and equipment, we simply returned to our normal production schedule without suffering serious damage, but it still took us a number of years to recover from the aftereffects. The kanten boom, I believe, only served to reaffirm the correctness of tree-ring management.

Think of Boom-Time Profits as a Temporary Trust

Looking back on it now, the fact that I had to engage

in management practices contrary to my own principles during the kanten boom makes me feel a little ashamed. From the standpoint of tree-ring management, I really should have avoided rapid growth. But I also learned another important lesson: booms are the greatest of misfortunes. This is not something I realized only after the boom had passed, but something I was already talking about with my employees as it was still in full swing.

The arrival of the boom brought a rapid increase in demand for kanten. This led all the kanten manufacturers to increase production, causing a sudden rise in the cost of the seaweed from which kanten is made. Ina Foods had no choice but to rely on such expensive raw material, which later became a drain on our finances.

It is as if the profits gained during the boom were simply depleted later. I kept my wits about me even in the midst of the boom, though, and not only avoided making any special capital investments, but also reminded myself that the money we were making was not really true profit.

A boom is like a wind at your back, but confusing the wind with your own skill can invite errors from which recovery is impossible. There are many managers who think they have things under control during normal times but lose sight of themselves when caught up in a boom.

Perhaps a golf analogy would be easiest to understand. You might find that the ball travels surprisingly far when aided by a tailwind, but it would be a mistake to congratulate yourself on the power of your tee shot. If you do, when faced with the sudden drop in the distance of your shot against a headwind, you'll struggle in disbelief and only work yourself into an even deeper slump.

The same is true in management. If you make the mistake of believing that progress under a tailwinds is the result of your own skill, you might be tempted to embark on excessive investments that come back to hurt you later. Still, anyone can make the right decision when the tailwind is obvious. The difficult part comes when it is unclear whether progress is being driven by a tailwind or by managerial skill. I think this requires managers to examine things very carefully, but in my experience, such situations almost always involve tailwinds.

How can I be so certain of this? Because Ina Foods began with almost no market at all for our products and worked slowly and steadily to create a market by expanding demand for kanten. We grew the market bit by bit back when there were neither booms nor tailwinds. Our company's rising income and rising profits over the course of half a century were achieved through our own hard work in slowly expanding the market. We know the difference between a tailwind and our own skill.

The arrival of the kanten boom, however, caused a sharp expansion of the market that led to all sorts of difficulties. One was the aforementioned rise in raw material costs. A bigger problem, though, was the flooding of the market by low-quality products seeking to cash in on the boom. This damaged the relationship of trust we had worked so long to cultivate with consumers. I believe the fact that the boom did not last was a result not only of the fickle nature of consumers who quickly turned to other health food products, but also of consumer frustration with low-quality products.

So what should you do when caught up in a boom? You cannot simply sit back and pretend it is not happening. I decided that the profits we made during the boom, since they had not been earned through efforts of our own, should be considered funds temporarily held in trust for someone else. By this, I mean that they should be seen as something the company will eventually have to give back.

On the other hand, I decided that any losses due to situations beyond our control, since they were lost through no fault or weakness of our own, should be considered held in trust by someone else. I believe that if we patiently pursue our business, take the long view, and keep tree-ring management as our ideal, the books will balance eventually.

Growth Is Employees Feeling Happier Than Before

There still seem to be a great many companies that subscribe to the doctrine of sales above all. Managers at such companies really believe that increasing sales is the only way to keep their companies growing. In extreme cases, they try to increase sales even if it means selling below cost and incurring losses.

I can certainly understand the argument that it is difficult to manage a company unless sales are expanding, yet I cannot help feeling there is something wrong with believing that increased sales are the same thing as corporate growth. Increasing sales only becomes a company's highest priority because the company equates increased sales with corporate growth. But surely it is an illusion to think that a large increase in sales means the company has grown tremendously.

Increased sales and increased profits are good news, but are increased sales and profits really the goal of management? Are they really proof of a company's growth? I believe that a company exists first and foremost to make its employees happy, and increasing sales and growing profits are nothing more than means of making employees happy.

The aim of tree-ring management is to be satisfied with sales and profits that are always a little better than the year before. It does not seek massive increases in sales or profits. What might be done in one year by grabbing an opportunity and working extremely hard should instead be achieved over two or three years of ordinary effort, because this better fosters the company's ability to endure.

I believe corporate growth is when employees have a real sense that, "Hey, things have gotten better. I'm happier than I was before." It is a gradual increase in the degree to which employees feel comfortable and happy. This is the proof that our company is growing; sales and profits are nothing more than means to this end.

There are surely many things that contribute to feeling happy, such as rising salaries, the sense that one's work is meaningful, and a more pleasant work environment. I think it is important to manage in a way that balances these goals with the need to ensure that the company endures.

When historians look back on our age 100 or 200 years from now, I am sure they will be amazed at how strange this era was: "They were awash in material goods and yet nobody was happy. So many companies were going bankrupt and so many people were struggling in poverty. What on Earth was going on?"

I am sure it will be no easy task to fix today's business world and its extremely off-balance pursuit of profits above all. And this is certainly caused in part by the way the stock market today measures the value of a company by its bottom line. This leaves some managers desperate to raise their company's stock price and market capitalization.

But I think now is the time to shift the course. To repeat: company growth is about employees feeling happier than they did before. It is important that more and more companies—each and every one counts—have the courage to make this adjustment and get back to fundamentals.

The economic recession is a huge test for those who manage companies. It is critical to take a close look at why your company exists and at what corporate growth really means. This is sure to bring a renewed understanding of where your company began and to encourage a return to basics. Returning to basics will reveal the way forward.

Profits Gained at the Expense of People Are Not Profits at All

There has recently been a growing shift toward management that prioritizes profit over sales. Of course, a reasonable degree of profit is indispensable in ensuring that a company endures. Over the last 10 years or so, pretax profits at Ina Foods have never fallen below 10% of sales. Unusual among small and medium-sized enterprises (SMEs), we have made annual investments of more than a billion yen (US $10 million) for over a decade, including investments in things other than production facilities and equipment.

It is certainly important to make a profit, and I often hear people say that it is only natural for management to seek profits. They have a point, but once profit becomes an end in itself, there is the risk of moving away from being a good company. Unless you are clear that profit is just a means of building a good company, it is easy to drift in the direction of improper management methods.

I cannot agree with the notion that the more profit one has, the better. The reason is that once you fall into believing in profit above all, it is far too easy to act as if anything is acceptable as long as it is profitable, and to forgo making even the expenditures that are necessary in order to secure further profits. The important aspects of profit are how it is generated and how it is used.

I constantly admonish myself that profits gained at the expense of people are not profits at all. For example, we do not apply undue pressure on suppliers to hold down the cost of the products they provide. That is, we purchase goods at a fair price, but we do not make unreasonable demands that would cause suppliers to take a loss.

The foundation of business is that both seller and buyer stand on equal ground. We earn a profit, but our partners must be able to earn a profit, too. When thinking only of one's own profit, it might make sense to squeeze the other party as far as they can be squeezed, but such relationships will not last very long.

Our company seeks to find value not in profit but in endurance. Therefore, we do not want to risk doing anything foolish, like losing a good trading partner for the sake of short-term profits. When we sell our products, too, we ask that they be bought at a fair price. If the other party's demands are unreasonable, we simply inform them that no deal is possible.

Although it is rather small, there is one other thing that Ina Foods has never compromised on: we apply our own revenue stamps to outgoing bills of exchange. This is the way it should be, of course, but it is a rule more frequently honored in the breach than the observance. When using a bill of exchange, the receiving party often ends up paying for the revenue stamp because the party that drafts the bill shifts to the recipient a cost that it should properly bear itself. Similarly, when making bank transfers, we always pay the transfer fee on our end. This, too, is as it should be, but there seem to be a great many companies that have the transfer fee deducted from the amount being transferred.

Revenue stamps and transfer fees are small costs, but they do add up. In order to reduce costs, therefore, many companies seek to have them carried by their trading partners. But this practice is not right. Even if such a company thinks it has gained something, it is actually advertising the fact that it is a company that makes unreasonable demands. The longer such practices continue, the longer the company promotes its own stinginess.

Within some companies, meanwhile, one often finds enthusiastic "rationalization" efforts underway—things like cutting personnel expenses, lowering the quality of employee welfare programs, and failing to make necessary workplace improvements—in the name of generating profits. Efforts to eliminate waste are necessary, but recently, there are an awful lot of companies that put profit first at the expense of their employees.

At our factories, 15-minute "tea breaks" are scheduled every day at 10 a.m. and 3 p.m. This is done out of consideration for the employees who work at our factories, in an effort to give them a proper rest. The company gives each person 500 yen (US $4.85) per month as a snack allowance. Some people also bring pickled vegetables or fresh fruit from home. I suppose these tea breaks would be seen as a waste by the rationalization camp, but they are very important from the standpoint of employee happiness.

Why do companies engage in short-term rationalization efforts that do not make their employees happier? I think this sort of thing probably begins as soon as a company sets short-term profit as its objective.

Profit Is Like Excrement Produced by a Healthy Body

Knowing how many managers place far too high a priority on profit, I often go out of my way to say things like, "Profit is the dregs—the dregs of management." Sometimes I use even earthier language and say, "You know, profit is crap." When I talk to managers like this, they always look at me strangely, but what I am getting at is what profit really amounts to.

Nobody makes defecation their goal in life, but any healthy body naturally produces excrement every day. Even without trying, out it comes. This is the key. Any healthy company should produce the excrement of profit as a matter of course. That's why, if you want to produce profit, you should think about building a healthy company. What does it mean for a company to be healthy? In a word, it means to be well balanced, just as it does with people.

A healthy person is neither too fat nor too skinny, with a fit, well-balanced body. Any company, too, with excessive subcutaneous or visceral fat can hardly be called healthy. At a company, body fat corresponds to internal reserves and extravagant systems. Saying "the more internal reserves one has, the better" is much like saying "the more fat one has, the better protected one is against starvation." Spending all one's time worried about starvation, however, can lead to lifestyle-related illnesses. But even more than that, being too fat makes the body less nimble. In the same way, companies, too, are at risk of becoming inactive and can even end up suffering from lifestyle-related illnesses.

On the other hand, not having enough fat leads to low immunity and a tendency toward sickliness. A company that has too few internal reserves is unable to weather even minor illnesses. In this way, is it important for both people and companies to maintain a balance.

A well-toned company is a powerful company. But just as a person who has only strong arms or only strong legs will be unbalanced, so a company needs to maintain balance in strengthening its manufacturing, sales, development, financial, and other muscles.

Furthermore, a healthy body enjoys good blood circulation and has nerves that are properly developed and reach all the way out to the extremities. In company terms, good blood circulation means an orderly internal chain of command that quickly conveys information and directives throughout the organization. Properly developed nerves mean that all employees are sensitive to the changes occurring in the world and are capable of responding quickly to them. Perhaps this could be called foresight.

It is probably easy enough for anyone to imagine a healthy body. With "balance" as the key word, all you have to do is substitute "company" for "body." For example, ask yourself whether a given company has a sales network commensurate with its size, or maintains proper research and development systems, or conducts thorough employee training. What about its contribution to the community, or to the environment? Is its level of name recognition commensurate with its size? The important thing is that these factors be balanced.

Just as a healthy body is well balanced, a healthy company is well balanced, too. And becoming even healthier leads to the company enduring. Unlike human beings, within companies people succeed one another in a kind of relay. The thing to do is to take the job or the company you are responsible for and seek to pass it on to the next person even healthier. The company as a whole grows healthier over time, and soon enough, it will be excreting profit as a matter of course.

Profit Itself Has No Value – What Is Important Is How It Is Used

There seem to be a great many companies that aim to be number one in something: if not number one in sales or number one in profits, then perhaps number one in Japan or number one in their industry. I sometimes find myself wondering whether the employees at such companies will be able to feel that they are the happiest in the world, or the happiest in Japan, or the happiest in their industry.

Believing as I do that sales and profits are nothing more than means for making employees happy, competing for position in terms of amount of sales or profits seems far removed from what a company really ought to be doing. To repeat: the goal a manager really ought to pursue is building a good company that contributes to society by making its employees happy.

I was born in 1937, so I suppose that unlike most people these days, I have some sense of what things were like before the end of the war. The education in morals that I received as a boy remains deeply ingrained. I was taught to work not only for my own sake, but also for the sake of the world and other people, and these values have stayed with me, unchanged.

Unfortunately, an excessive emphasis on respect for the individual and individual liberty under the post-war educational system has led to the disappearance of a moral duty to work "for the world and for others." Recently a growing number of people seem to think that anything goes as long as things come out all right for them, or that it is acceptable to do wrong as long as nobody finds out. I cannot help thinking that this trend feeds into the doctrine of profit above all.

Profit itself has no value; value is generated in the way profit is used. The most important issue for a manager is the matter of how to use profits. For a manager, making such decisions requires asking what the company exists to achieve and what kind of company he wants to make it. I try to use profits to increase employee happiness. This is not as easy as simply raising their salaries. Exorbitant bonuses in the short term make it impossible for the company to endure, and defeat the entire purpose. Rather, raising salaries each year, even if only a little at a time, increases employees' sense of happiness.

Our annual investments in excess of one billion yen (US $10 million) over the last decade have been applied to more than just building up our production capacity. A substantial portion has been directed to bettering the workplace environment by turning our headquarters grounds into a park, making improvements to office buildings, and bolstering welfare programs. We want employees to feel that their workplace has become more comfortable than the year before.

Management from other companies might think we would be better off investing such funds in cutting-edge factories and equipment, but I chose instead to construct a new office building to replace our old, cramped facility and to turn our grounds into a park. Beginning 40 years ago, we have organized company-subsidized employee trips overseas every other year.

In addition, as a means of giving back to the community, we built a pedestrian bridge that could be used by students on their way to and from school, and also constructed a private road alongside the public road, which we are entitled to use, in order to prevent traffic congestion.

We have maintained sponsorships of events such as traditional Noh and Kyogen performances for the enjoyment of local residents as well as of the Saito Kinen

Festival conducted by Seiji Ozawa. We have also sponsored the Spring High School Ekiden Relay Race in Ina since 1992, when it was still just a minor event; recently it has become a huge event drawing 140 schools from around the country. These are just a few examples of the community service activities that Ina Foods engages in, but they all share the characteristic of making a long-term commitment once we have become involved.

Fortunately, Ina Foods has enjoyed rising income and rising profits for half a century. To be sure, rising income and profits are what enable us to make such commitments, but I also believe that long-term commitments lead to a measure of success. This is why the stability gained through tree-ring management is so important.

Aim to Be a Company That Gathers Moss

At Ina Foods, we have turned the grounds of our headquarters into a natural park space called Kanten Papa Gardens that anyone is free to use. The area contains a forest of red pines, and our improvement efforts began from a desire to leave as many of the old trees behind as we could.

The roughly 100,000-square-meter grounds make use of the natural terrain and include our headquarters, R&D center, and other facilities, as well as Kanten Papa

Hall, a gallery housing a permanent art collection; a Japanese-style kanten restaurant called Satsuki-tei; a Western-style kanten restaurant called Himawari-tei; and Sun Flora, a shop that sells imported interior goods.

Kanten Papa Gardens is surrounded by abundant greenery, and just walking through the area feels like taking a recreational stroll. The rolling paths through the trees lead to the restaurants and shop. By incorporating deep eaves and other elements of traditional Japanese residential architecture, the office buildings have been designed to blend in with the surrounding scenery. Roughly 350,000 people visit Kantan Papa Gardens each year. There are no guards at the gate; people are free to come and go as they please.

We began developing Kanten Papa Gardens in 1987, during a time when everyone was giddy with the bubble economy and Japanese companies were all heading in the direction of expansion and growth. I had no intention, though, of vainly pursuing an expansion of sales or profits.

I tried to think of ways we could make a more comfortable workplace environment for our employees and increase their satisfaction. I felt sure that if we could create a pleasant workplace surrounded in greenery, it would please our employees and make them happy. I was confident, too, that doing so would also contribute to beautifying the local townscape. This was my motivation for creating Kanten Papa Gardens.

More than 30 years have passed since then. Careful tending by our employees has made Kanten Papa Gardens better with each passing day. Our employees themselves even inject the red pines with pesticides to protect them from bark beetle infestation. Our workday begins at 8:20, but most employees arrive by about 7:50 and take part in tending or tidying up Kanten Papa Gardens. This is not something the company requires; employees come on their own initiative to do this work. Customers arrive on weekends and holidays, too, and there is almost always someone around tending the grounds. When time allows, I like to show up and lead everyone in tending the plants.

Many customers, it seems, see the gardens and think, "What a good company." With 350,000 visitors a year, this makes for unparalleled publicity. Local people are impressed to learn that employees voluntarily tend the gardens every morning. I am very pleased to think that in some small way, this contributes to raising our stature in the local community.

I actually have an even grander plan. The ground beneath our red pines is now covered with a wide expanse of grass, but one day, I would like to see it covered with moss instead. I want us to be a company that "gathers moss." I have conveyed this to our employees and the moss is already beginning to grow.

I make jokes, saying, "Hey, you could look all around Japan and not find another company that gathers moss. We could be the only one in Japan!" But this notion of being a company that gathers moss is serious. Moss only grows where there are trees, which means taking care of the environment. Moss also only grows in areas that are carefully tended, and it grows only very slowly. This ties into thinking about endurance and being careful in pursuing the tasks that every day brings. I hope we truly will become a company that gathers moss.

Ten Rules for Building a Good Company

Ina Foods has established 10 rules for building a good company. These outline the principles for achieving steady and reliable corporate growth, similar to the layering of tree rings. I listed these rules below. Their content is so ordinary readers may wonder what all the fuss is about.

But think for a moment about whether all of these things are being consistently carried out at your own company. It is no easy task to continue doing the perfectly ordinary in a consistent way. That is why I compiled these 10 rules in writing, so we could always refer to them and keep ourselves in line.

Ten Rules for Building a Good Company

1. Always produce good products.
2. Do not produce too much or sell too much just because you can.
3. Seek whenever possible to sell at a fixed price without offering discounts.
4. Seek to produce products and services from the customer perspective.
5. Create beautiful factories, shops, and gardens.
6. Develop refined packaging and advertisements.
7. Give back to the community by volunteering and by supporting culture and the arts.
8. Take care of suppliers.
9. Improve the company image by ensuring that everyone understands management policies.
10. Carry out the above faithfully over time.

As you can see by reading these 10 rules, there is nothing particularly new about any of them, yet consistently carrying out all of these perfectly ordinary rules leads to a fresh, new company. Indeed, I think of these 10 rules as the know-how for branding our company.

The word "branding" may cause some to wonder if I intend to turn Kanten Papa into Louis Vuitton. But what I mean by a "brand" is nothing other than a trusted company gaining customers by producing trusted products. A good brand has good fans.

Surely no one goes into a Louis Vuitton shop and haggles over price. Their customers are satisfied to purchase expensive products. And the people at Louis Vuitton work hard to ensure that the products they make are satisfying even at high prices. This is the kind of business to which I aspire, and this is what I mean by "branding."

Look around the world, though, and one sees a flood of phrases like "rock bottom prices," "discount king," and "price slashing." But do businesses based on "low, low prices" really benefit consumers? The consumers who purchase products are also the employees of the companies that sell them. Selling at a fair price generates profits for the company that provides the products, which then increases the purchasing power of its employees.

If both sellers and suppliers make a reasonable profit, and if these profits are used not only to make their companies bigger but are also distributed reasonably to employees, then domestic consumption, which accounts for

60% of Japan's GDP, will naturally grow. In this way, the securing and distribution of reasonable profits is critical for improving the economy through the promotion of domestic consumption.

Branding ties into ensuring the ability to secure a reasonable profit, and is the key to corporate endurance. Put another way, branding—that is, gaining customers by producing trusted products—is management itself. It might be impossible to fully develop our brand in my time, and perhaps not even in the time of my successor, but I think there is no better time to start than the present.

CHAPTER 2

Creating a Company That Makes Employees Happy

Personnel Expenses Are Not a Cost, But the Very Goal of the Company

Some time ago, there was a popular aphorism that went, "When we all cross against a red light together, there is nothing to fear." Apt in its way, I cannot help feeling that the saying is especially on target in describing a recent tendency I have seen among company managers. Indeed, it is as if they have decided that if everyone crosses against the red, then doing so is correct.

I am referring specifically to the cutting of personnel expenses. In simplest terms, the only ways to raise profits are to increase sales or to lower expenses. During times when consumption is stagnant, cutting expenses can seem like the most efficient means of raising profits.

In fact, after the collapse of Japan's bubble economy, companies whose performance dropped rushed to cut away unprofitable divisions in the name of "selection and consolidation." There is nothing wrong with getting rid of unprofitable divisions, but these companies were also quick to do away with the people in those divisions at the same time.

And it did not end there. Managers who felt it was imperative to execute a V-shaped recovery began taking every possible step to reduce personnel expenses. With no regard to labor intensification, they lowered personnel numbers and began to switch from regular to temporary employees. The ironic result was that more and more people in society grew unhappy even as corporate performance recovered.

Companies that embarked on cost-cutting efforts and major restructuring were rewarded in the stock market with rising share prices. Because reducing personnel expenses—a fixed cost—does make an enormous contribution to lowering costs and increasing profits overall, many other companies followed suit by trying to lower their expenses. It seemed to me that everyone was "crossing against the red together." Suddenly, a red light meant that you had to cross.

The situation only grew worse. During the recession, Japanese corporations all rushed to lay off their non-regular employees, and did so with no apparent sense of shame, acting as if this were a perfectly normal means of reducing personnel expenses and cutting costs. They strode proudly as they crossed against the red.

I do not think of personnel expenses as a cost; personnel expenses are the goal. Imagine that you have started a business with siblings or close friends. In that situation, would anyone think it was a good idea to keep personnel costs as low as possible? I doubt it. After all, one of the reasons for starting the company was surely to work hard, earn more money, and become happier together.

What is the point of starting a company if you have to reduce people's pay in order to increase profits? I suppose the situation might be different for publicly-listed companies, but for the average small or medium-sized enterprise, there is no problem at all if, after the company has used the resources that it should use and paid people what they should be paid, nothing remains by way of profits. As long as the company is spending what it should to ensure that it endures, there is no shame in having no profit left over once resources have been used and salaries paid.

This is the reason I say, "Profits are dregs." Why bother accumulating a huge pile of dregs? If a company acts properly to use the resources and make the payments it should, it ought to be capable of enduring. I believe this is the correct way to think about unlisted small and medium-sized enterprises. If you want to increase profits, you should first think about how to increase the added value offered by your products and services, then build a system that ensures you can sell them at a fair price.

Unfortunately, the recent trend seems to be to neglect the labor-intensive process of increasing added value in favor of the quick and easy path of cutting costs. Downsizing is probably the most conspicuous example. Ina

Foods has never engaged in downsizing. I believe that the concept of downsizing as a tool of last resort—one to be used only when all other alternatives have been pursued—is perhaps the most fundamental ethical principle that managers should hold.

Corporate Tax Is Not the Only Tax

From the perspective of the manager who pursues nothing but short-term profit, the expenses necessary to pay employees, to provide for their welfare, to support culture and the arts, and to make a contribution to the local community all begin to seem like nothing but costs. As I have already mentioned, I believe this to be a mistake.

Still, the trend in the world seems to be to look positively upon "cutting expenses." It is important, of course, to eliminate waste, but managers who cut even the expenses that are necessary for the company to endure will end up wringing their own necks over the long term.

I call this the start of a "vicious cycle of stinginess." What happens when you get stingy about personnel and employee welfare expenses? Employee morale almost always drops. A drop in employee morale means a drop in corporate vitality, and could even mean an increase in workplace accidents. In any case, the result is a drop in corporate performance.

What happens if salaries start to actually fall? Employees become reluctant to open their wallets. When they stop buying things, consumption drops. Since consumer spending accounts for 60% of Japan's GDP, flagging consumption causes a decline in the Japanese economy. What goes around, comes around, and soon enough, there will be a negative impact on your company's performance, too.

Eliminating support for culture, the arts, and activities that contribute to the community means that those who were involved in such projects will have to curtail the scope of their activities, which inevitably has a chilling effect on the economy.

In this way, when your company starts getting stingy about its expenditures, it contributes to a pullback by the economy as a whole that ultimately leads to a worsening of your company's performance. In turn, this leads to a new round of efforts to cut costs even further. The stingier your company becomes, the worse the economy gets, which only makes things tougher for yourself. You become trapped in a vicious cycle. The problem is that everyone tends to think that stinginess by their own company alone will have no effect—that other companies will somehow pick up the slack.

The same can be said of expenses designed to make the workplace more comfortable. Employees spend a huge portion of their lives at their company, so an uncomfortable workplace leads to lower morale and a drop in efficiency. Many managers seek short-term profits by making cuts in this area, but I think this has a negative effect on employees. In a workplace that always grows more unpleasant, no matter how much managers may urge employees to work harder, they will have a difficult time imagining a brighter future.

One area where care must be taken is investment in research and development. When management runs into difficulties, it is tempting to try and rein in research and development costs, as if choosing to "eat the rice today rather than plant it to grow more rice tomorrow." From the perspective of managing from the long view, this is suicidal. There is a need for balance, but you cannot become so caught up in chasing short-term profits that you neglect to sow the seeds of the business's future. If you do, the company will be unable to endure.

If there really are no profits, then cutting R&D costs may be unavoidable (although in that case, you really ought to first set about developing a management strategy that generates profits), but skimping on necessary expenses in order to generate profits invites a vicious cycle that will ultimately threaten your company's ability to endure. I do not know whether it is out of consideration for shareholders or simply a desire to look good, but there seem to be an awful lot of managers who cling stubbornly to profits.

When it comes to paying taxes, too, there seem to be a great many managers who seem to think they have done something outstanding when they pay a great deal of corporate income tax. For my part, as long as I am going to pay taxes, I would much prefer to spend the same amount on employee income taxes withheld by the company. Because corporate taxes have fallen and income taxes have risen, our company still pays roughly the same amount to the national government.

Instead of being stingy with personnel expenses, I think it is better to pay the highest salaries we can and have the tax delivered to the government in the form of income tax. This is better for employees, better for the company, and better for society. And when income is used for consumption, it increases consumption tax revenues, too.

Instead of focusing on short-term profits or making management look good, it is better to take the long view and aim to use profits in ways that generate virtuous cycles.

Maintain Internal Harmony Through a System of Seniority by Length of Service

I do not favor the sort of human resources systems that have become popular lately, such as performance-based pay and wages based on ability. The wage system at Ina Foods is based primarily on seniority by length of service. Out-of-order promotions do happen, but they are not the norm.

When there is no particular difference in ability, older employees and employees who have been with the company longer are paid higher wages. There has been no major employee dissatisfaction with this. Rather, employees support the system because it enables them to feel peace of mind in approaching their work.

When you adopt performance-based pay or salaries based solely on ability, you inevitably end up evaluating individual performance. Even if you expand the scope of evaluation a bit, you are still looking at teams or departments.

Let us assume for a moment that a certain individual or a certain team performs in a manner that truly stands out. Was that performance really achieved only as a result of that individual or team? Surely others provided support. In most cases, it is a flower that has blossomed only as the result of accumulated efforts over a long period of time. Perhaps management resources were used that had been accumulated by the company. The company's reputation, cultivated over many years, probably played a significant part. Most of all, somebody must have nurtured that individual or team.

A human resources system that sets all those factors aside and gives preferential treatment only to those who happen to be there when the results come in seems wrong to me. I cannot approve of a system that tries to make employees run faster by dangling money before their noses like carrots.

A company is a community that shares a common purpose. I would even go so far as to say it is a family. Indeed, employees at my company often refer to themselves as the Ina Foods family. Just because a younger brother is strong and works hard, do his father and older brother reduce their own portions of rice to feed the younger brother more? Surely it would not please the younger brother were they to do so. Aren't things happier when all members of the family do their best, each contributing what he can, sharing both the responsibility and rewards together?

When you adopt performance-based pay or salaries that emphasize individual assessment, people become interested only in short-term numbers. They place a higher priority on their own performance than on cooperating with others. In extreme cases, they may even take joy in a neighboring employee's performance slump. A culture develops in which it becomes acceptable to disregard experienced employees whose performance is poor.

This is no way to maintain a harmonious company. I am certainly not saying that everyone needs to be the closest of friends. Indeed, it is much preferable that employees engage in heated debate in the pursuit of true corporate growth. However, a company is capable of exerting its greatest power when everyone on the inside is united in working together. Performance-based pay and salaries based on ability run the risk of chipping away at the company's ability to make this kind of united effort. I cannot help thinking that the recent trend toward being concerned only about oneself, or only about the present, is related to the spread of performance-based pay and salaries based on ability.

There is one other reason I prefer the system of seniority by length of service. When you consider the life cycle of getting married, having children, and sending children to school, people in their 40s and 50s face mounting expenses. Performance-based pay gives no consideration to an individual's life situation in evaluating his work performance, but I think this approach is shortsighted.

As the old saying goes, "Even a sparrow may hatch an eagle's egg." That is, even ordinary parents sometimes raise magnificent children. We must avoid a situation in which a talented child is unable to receive an adequate education because the performance-based pay of his parents is too low. This would be a loss to the nation.

It may sound overly dramatic, but as someone who was forced to leave his own academic aspirations unfulfilled, I want all children to have an equal opportunity to receive an education regardless of whether their parents are eagles or sparrows. The system of seniority by length of service serves this end.

The Greatest Source of Efficiency Is Motivation Born From a Sense of Happiness

When I say that I do not introduce performance-based pay or salaries based on ability, many managers will wonder how we manage to motivate employees. Performance-based pay and salaries based on ability, though, cannot really motivate people in the truest sense. Young people today, unlike those of my generation, do not have a strong desire for money or position.

I think only a surprisingly small number of employees would think we had done the right thing if we were to introduce performance-based pay or salaries based on ability. In times like these, there simply is not enough room for so many people to receive exceptionally high salaries or to jump quickly up the ladder. Even for those who did well over the short term, it would not last.

Rather, I think most people would end up managed strictly and impersonally, feeling that they were being driven by a slap on the backside. What they are looking for is a workplace where they can freely pursue their work in an environment of peaceful interpersonal relationships. I think this trend among young people will continue.

This does not, however, mean the company should coddle them. The only people the company needs are those who can exercise control over themselves, always maintaining a desire to improve and a willingness to take on new challenges. This is much more difficult than traditional notions of management and impossible to accomplish without sustaining a high level of employee motivation.

I believe employees are motivated not by money or position but rather by their sense that through their work, things are better—and they are happier—this year than last year. When one is part of a company where one feels happier this year than last year, and where next year promises to be better still, motivation rises naturally.

This is why it is so important for managers to find ways to ensure that employees feel happier—even if only a little bit happier—this year than the year before. Employees gain no peace of mind from having their salaries shoot up one year only to fall sharply the next. Won't they feel happier if their salaries rise every year, even if only a little bit at a time?

The same is true of the work environment. The reason we decided to build Kanten Papa Gardens was that I was convinced that tending the grounds every year would create a sense of the work environment getting better and better, which was sure to make employees feel happy, too.

For office spaces, we have always built facilities that were perhaps just a little bit more lavish than our actual needs at the time, taking care to ensure that the amount of space available for each person's use would increase even if we added more employees. We always make sure to place the employee dining room in the best location in the building. If even such trivial efforts lead to happier employees, there is no reason not to put them into action. They also deepen employee affection for their company and workplace.

At Ina Foods, we offer a substantial lending program

for employees. We hope that if they find themselves short of funds, they will consult with us first before rushing off to consumer credit companies. We also provide an in-house savings program, offering interest rates that are slightly higher than other financial institutions. Most employees, I think, deposit the maximum possible amount.

These programs give employees a sense of security and play a role in boosting motivation. Raising the motivation of employees in this way is actually the greatest source of efficiency in management, even more effective than introducing the latest equipment.

The thing you must never forget is that people, especially young people, have a deep-seated sense of justice. If the company or its managers engage in unethical activity, then employee motivation will surely fall. On the other hand, if employees believe that what they are doing is for the sake of the world and for others, then they will try their best to work hard even when things are rough. Employees will gladly follow a manager who demonstrates the courage to reform an unjust world.

Don't Switch Suppliers Just Because Another One Is Cheaper

Making sure the company endures is only one of the

fundamentals of my management approach; another is continuity. I have already mentioned how once we begin making donations to activities that contribute to the community, we seldom stop.

This is perfectly natural, of course, but even the smallest things become enormously powerful when done continuously over time. Needless to say, you must be careful, because continuity in doing something incorrectly only compounds the problem. Continuity in doing the right thing, however, creates tremendous power.

At Ina Foods, we almost never change suppliers. We certainly don't switch suppliers frequently by always searching for the lowest price. Rather, we try to respect those suppliers with whom we have been fortunate enough to start a relationship. We send them mid-year and year-end presents and never ask for unreasonable discounts.

I suspect some might think this means we operate with high supplier costs, but that is not the case at all. When we treat others well, they treat us well in return. First of all, we do not do business with the sort of companies that would see us as an easy mark and try to take us for a ride. It is important to develop a relationship of trust before beginning to trade with one another. We carefully consider whether the company is one with which we can develop a long-term relationship. We do not pounce right away just because a company offers the lowest price.

Indeed, you cannot really call it business unless you are able to develop a relationship in which both sides prosper through long-term fidelity. Demanding that a supplier sell below cost may seem like a good idea in the short term, but it does more harm than good over time. The supplier will surely bear feelings of mistrust toward you, while also putting pressure on its own suppliers. What happens as this continues down the chain? You will see the vicious cycle begin.

To repeat: profits gained at the expense of others are not true profits. Profits gained by making unreasonable demands of suppliers are also not true profits. I want our relationships with suppliers to enable both sides to enjoy ongoing prosperity over the long term. Strangely enough, when we adopt this approach, suppliers begin to wish for our prosperity in return.

Deciding not to switch suppliers easily is something I learned from watching the way long-established companies are managed. Companies that have been around for a century or two have accumulated a great deal of wisdom. Based on what I learned from a number of long-established companies that I respect, I distilled five conditions for becoming the sort of company that could join their ranks:

1. Do not grow too fast.
2. Do not switch suppliers just because another one is cheaper.
3. Do not cut personnel.
4. Constantly incorporate improved production methods and materials.
5. Always think about what can be done to please the customers.

When presented in this way, you can see that there is a great deal of overlap with the core parts of my own management philosophy. Indeed, it would not be overstating the case to say that becoming a long-established company is the aim of my management approach.

I would hate to be misunderstood, so let me emphasize that continuity is not the same thing as never changing. The best of the long-established companies do not simply rest on the laurels of their venerable brands; they constantly incorporate the latest manufacturing technology, ingredients, sales methods, and management techniques to cope with change over time. Indeed, this is what has made their continuity possible. Continuity can only be achieved through an accumulation of innovations that meet the needs of changing times.

A Relationship of Trust Is More Important Than a Contract

I have been able to learn a great many things through dealing with people from long-established companies, including some that have been around for more than 500 years. I have often been impressed at the insight of such companies.

For example, long-established companies never think about closing up shop under their current generation of management. They always think about the next generation, and the next, and so on, forever. They are committed to developing slowly over time rather than producing spectacular results on their own watch.

This is why long-established companies never make growth their primary aim and never downsize their employees. They never produce inferior products and always take care of their customers, because they hope their current customers' children, and then their children, too, will someday become customers as well.

There is a manager at one such long-established company with whom I have had a friendship—outside of work—for more than 25 years. Both of us would like to enter into a business relationship at some point, but I have never asked him to buy our products, and he has never offered, and all of a sudden 25 years had passed.

Commercial relationships are founded on quality products, but simply having good products is not enough. When I say this, many people may assume that the next priority is price, but I believe there is something even more important than price: a relationship of trust with the party with whom you will be doing business.

When deciding between a lower-priced supplier with whom I have no relationship of trust and a slightly higher-priced supplier with whom I do have such a relationship, I will choose the latter, because I believe trust is more important than price. I think this is the reason why long-established companies do not readily switch suppliers.

How do you go about building a relationship of trust? Of course you must understand the other party's personality and attitude, but merely being on friendly terms is not enough to establish trust. The important thing, I think, is to be bound by a proper philosophy of business or management, that is, to share a common philosophy. Only then can one say that a relationship of commercial trust has been built.

In the course of my dealings with long-established

companies, I have come to hope that over time we might develop a relationship of trust that leads to a commercial relationship. If this does not happen in my generation, or the next, or the next after that, it is all right. But once a relationship of trust has been built, it becomes a bond stronger than any contract, because both parties have come to an agreement and feel confident in the shared desire to develop further together.

Looking at today's economy, everyone is so intent on chasing short-term numbers that no one has any time left to think about other things. Even though the economy has developed, culture has not. In long-established companies, management and culture are united. The families who run long-established companies have produced many refined people who have contributed to raising the level of Japanese culture. This improves the image of the company and even has an influence on its management.

Long-established companies have an air of culture; there is no such company that lacks culture. Perhaps this is another secret to corporate endurance. Culture brings us joy and enriches our lives. A company that ignores culture and measures itself only by economic efficiency might as well announce that it cares little for the enrichment and happiness of its employees, community, and society.

It is difficult to carry on supporting art, cultural, and sporting activities during a recession, but I believe it is necessary to follow the example of long-established companies and provide enrichment and joy through culture.

Do Not Get Involved in Deals Beyond Your Capabilities

In 1980, Ina Foods launched products for home use under the brand Kanten Papa. Today, the Kanten Papa brand encompasses a lineup of more than 200 products, but many readers have probably never seen any of them. The reason is that Kanten Papa products only appear on store shelves in our home prefecture of Nagano and in some areas of neighboring Yamanashi prefecture. For the most part, they are sold directly to consumers by mail order.

We have continued to rely on this sales method because I believe it is best not to get involved in deals beyond our capabilities. In the past, we have had opportunities to rapidly expand sales volume, but chose not to take them.

This is an old story. The Kanten Papa lineup includes a popular product called Cup Jelly 80°C that launched in 1981. Dissolved in water at 80°C and left at room temperature, the product turns to jelly, which tastes even better when chilled in the refrigerator. The simplicity of the product has made it a huge hit. It now comes in 10 different flavors, including orange, green apple, grapefruit, grape, and coffee.

After Cup Jelly 80°C hit the market, a major supermarket chain approached us with an offer to roll out the product nationwide. If it were made available through a big-name supermarket, Cup Jelly 80°C would surely become a major product overnight. Sales would skyrocket, and Kanten Papa would suddenly become a household name.

Almost all of our executives were in favor of selling through the supermarket. At the board of directors meeting, everyone said, "We have to do this." But after thinking about it very carefully, I turned the offer down. I decided it was simply beyond the capability of Ina Foods at the time.

A nationwide rollout would have required us to hire temporary workers and rapidly build additional production facilities. There was a real possibility that we might find ourselves unable to maintain adequate quality control. Stretching excessively in the pursuit of short-term profits has a tendency to be a source of trouble in the future. Without prospects for a sufficient follow-through, I decided the deal was too much of a stretch and called it off.

I also considered the fact that if one distribution channel were to grow too large, the company would inevitably come to depend on it, and the company would become more difficult to manage in a balanced way. This worried me. In today's terms, I thought about risk hedging. I decided that even though it would take time, I would engage in balanced management by developing a variety of products in different domains, distributing production bases in different locations, and developing a variety of sales channels.

Fortunately, our company now handles more than 1,000 products that are sold in a broad range of industries, including food products, food service, cosmetics, and pharmaceuticals. We have retail shops of our own and a growing mail-order business that operates through the Internet and other sales channels.

At our company, we aim to sell with no returns. With food products, there is no other option but to incinerate goods that go unsold or are past their expiration date. As wasteful as it may be, such products must be burned as garbage. Not only is this a loss from a management perspective, it can also be seen as a waste of resources that has a negative impact on the environment and must be avoided whenever possible. In this way, too, tree-ring management has been a source of great strength.

Better to Sell Well Than Sell a Lot

The sales route for products in Japan typically, in simplest terms, runs "manufacturer → wholesaler → retailer." This system is sustained by ensuring that everyone secures a reasonable profit.

Today, however, Japan seems to have become a market-based economy that worships competition and makes it difficult to secure a reasonable profit. Manufacturers, wholesalers, and retailers alike are all gasping for air under excessive competition that goes beyond reducing profits to selling below cost.

I suspect times are tough for everyone during such a major recession, but I cannot help thinking that if things continue on as they are, we will all be the poorer for it. This may be laughed off as a fantasy, but what would happen if every company raised its terms of purchase by 10%—every manufacturer, every wholesaler, and every retailer? In response, this would mean that every company would simultaneously raise its prices by 10%. This would never happen, of course, but what if it did? In broad terms, it would lead to an increase of 10% in the added value of the Japanese economy. Doesn't this paint a more appealing picture than clumsy government methods of dealing with the recession?

Even setting aside such grand daydreams, the excessive

competition that causes companies to sell below their own cost is a threat to those companies' ability to endure. This is why I believe it is more important to sell well than to sell a lot. I have already written about how our company does not make unreasonable demands for discounts because we believe that suppliers have a right to make a profit, too.

Turning things around, we believe we also have a right to make a profit and want our buyers to recognize this. I tell our sales representatives that if buyers make outrageous demands or try to force unreasonable terms, it is perfectly all right to turn them down, even if it is a large-volume deal.

Some time ago, a new purchasing agent took charge at one of our major client companies and demanded that we sell at a lower price than the one we had arranged with his predecessor. It seemed to us that the new fellow was trying to force a discount in order to boost his own performance. We were doing a substantial business with the company at the time, but decided we had no choice but to stop trading with them.

Taking the position that "We're doing you a favor by buying your products, so we're on top" is simply wrong. I repeat, as a reminder to myself too, that in business, the seller and the buyer ought to stand on equal footing.

Both should prosper together. Deals that depend on the buyer unreasonably leveraging its purchasing power will not turn out well over the long term.

"Selling well" means securing a reasonable profit. Consumers today want more than just the lowest price. I think they want to feel satisfied with a company's approach to business and want a company to be able to steadily supply products of consistently high quality. They will happily purchase such products without haggling for a discount.

One manager I know told me that after hearing me speak, he put an end to his own store's "sales first" approach of selling large volumes at low prices and made the shift to "selling well." He also did away with meaningless freebies and extra services. The result, he told me, is that profits, which had been falling every year, have stabilized.

Excessive discounting and unnecessary services impoverish a business. Customers who pounce initially will gradually grow accustomed to them and start to seek new and greater incentives. Needless to say, there are limits when you go to extremes, and what lies at the extremes is the demise of the company.

Even if things are more difficult over the short term, selling good products at a fair price is still the best option over the long term. This is management that takes the long view.

The Roots of Profit Lie in Creating Markets with New Products and Increasing Share

When I joined Ina Foods, there was almost no market for kanten at all, and I was concerned about whether we would be able to make a go of it in the kanten industry. Not only were we behind the curve technologically, we were also short of funds. It was a situation that did little to encourage optimism.

In any case, we had no choice but to conjure up demand for kanten on our own. We started off by making sweets using kanten and trying to sell the idea to confectionery manufacturers. Ever since, Ina Foods has engaged in an exhaustive search for new applications for kanten. I call this "deep plowing." Kanten is basically nothing more than the result of boiling down tengusa or ogonori seaweed and then hardening the extract into stick, strand, or powder forms. Deep plowing opens up infinite possibilities even for such simple substances.

For example, we once manufactured a kind of kanten that would not harden. Although it was the result of a mistake during production, we thought it might be useful for something. After developing techniques for producing this "mistake" in volume, we found ways to use it in cosmetics and nursing care food as a "soft" kanten. We made beverages, too. Today, this low-coagulation product, dubbed "ultra kanten," is used widely in a variety of applications.

Through joint research conducted with Professor Osamu Tochikubo at the Yokohama City University School of Medicine, we discovered that ingesting 180 grams of kanten jelly prior to meals is effective in improving metabolic syndrome. Based on this research, we began to develop kanten products for use as part of a metabolic diet.

By continuing such deep plowing, our company has already obtained 60 patents, with many more patents pending. We have more than 1000 products serving a wide array of markets, including confectionery manufacturers, the food service industry, and pharmaceutical manufacturers. Our line of Kanten Papa products for household use has grown to account for fully 40% of sales.

From early on, we aimed to be a company founded on research and development. Perhaps it would be more accurate to say that R&D was our only path to survival; after all, there were no existing markets. By digging deeply into a single ingredient, we have managed to build ties with all sorts of customers in a variety of industries.

Our company's strength lies in its ability to develop new products and create new markets on our own. This is why our products have a high market share. It is what keeps us from being exposed to futile price wars and ties into our ability to secure a reasonable profit.

But our company also has one other strength: for the most part, we have always manufactured the production equipment installed at our factories ourselves. As the machines have grown larger in recent years, we are now more likely to place orders with outside equipment manufacturers, but we can still make smaller equipment in-house. We have mechanical engineering experts on staff for this purpose, and at its peak, our mechanical engineering division had around 20 employees.

This enabled us to create all sorts of original production equipment that prevented competitors from easily copying us when we rolled out a successful product. Having a mechanical engineering division has also greatly improved our ability to maintain our equipment. If anything breaks, we can fix it right away, and it is easy to make upgrades. This led to a higher uptime ratio for our factories.

Making our own production equipment generated an enormous competitive advantage for our company. But it all began because we were unable to buy equipment due to lack of funds in the early days.

Even when funds are limited, wisdom is boundless. This is why I like to describe business as a game of wits.

Believing That People Are Inherently Good Lowers Costs

Many Japanese companies seem to engage in management grounded in the notion that people are inherently evil. This is why they constrain their employees with regulations and supervise them in the name of "evaluation." When relationships with suppliers and customers are built on the presumption that people are inherently evil, you must be constantly alert for any potential wrongdoing. When it comes to collecting bills, for example, you may have to head out on the due date to accept payment yourself. Such things incur enormous costs.

Conversely, if you manage from the perspective that people are inherently good, you can lower costs considerably. Eliminating the need to keep constant watch over every little thing your employees do drastically lowers the cost of running your administrative division, and it also reduces personnel expenses. Being sufficiently connected to both suppliers and customers through relationships of trust can eliminate a great deal of unnecessary time and trouble.

An example I often give is the difference between European railroads and those in Japan. In Japan, your ticket is checked when you pass through the gate and then again after you have boarded the train. In the Green Car and on express trains, a conductor passes through every time the train stops at a station to check if anyone new has come on board.

In Europe, on the other hand, with the exception of high-speed rail, tickets are almost never checked. The check at the gate is merely perfunctory. Apparently there are severe penalties for riding without paying one's fare, but most passengers purchase the correct ticket as a matter of conscience. From what I am told, the number of people who ride without paying is small and has a negligible impact on operating costs.

You could say that the railroads in Japan operate on the assumption that people are inherently evil, while in Europe they operate on the assumption that people are inherently good. Even when charging the same fare, operating on the assumption that people are inherently good will make it possible to redirect those resources from checking tickets to providing other services.

At our company, for example, employees have the authority to act on their own initiative if they think it will help improve customer service. If visitors to Kanten

Papa Gardens have difficulty walking, for example, on-site employees can choose to call a taxi for them or even drive them to or from the station. I do not worry that the staff might use this as an excuse to skip work because I take the view that people are inherently good and I have confidence in our employees.

We do not have security guards at Kanten Papa Gardens, either. Anyone can come and go as he pleases. The well water on site is available for anyone to draw as much as he wants. This is because we trust our customers, and so far, there has been no problems. The lovely gardens we built would surely be worth only half as much if we were suspicious of visitors and restricted them from enjoying it.

These are trivial examples, but Ina Foods is grounded in the belief that people are inherently good. When people are trusted, they become filled with the desire to live up to that trust. Conversely, those who are viewed with suspicion feel awful about not being trusted. It goes without saying which mindset is better for the company.

We try to take this same approach in our relationships with our trading partners as well. In 2008, we built a new, five-story R&D center. We did not put out a call for bids; we hired architects and contractors we had worked with before. We engage in some sort of construction nearly every year and always hire the same companies to do the work. We trust them and leave everything in their hands. We do not worry about the possibility that they might charge unfair prices or cut corners. Indeed, because of our long-term relationship with them, they are far more likely to make an extra effort to build something good without regard for their own profit.

To tell the truth, there is a secret underlying our company's ability to manage from the position that people are inherently good: education. You cannot manage in this way unless both management and employees adopt the correct mindset through education. This is why I believe that managers have to be educators, a topic I will address in detail in Chapter Four.

Do Not Go Public: Settling Accounts Once Every Three Years Is Enough

About 15 years ago, I looked into the idea of taking our company public. I spoke to several people and listened carefully to their suggestions, but in the end, I decided against it. I cannot dismiss the possibility that some later generation of management might decide to go public, but I determined that it would not happen during my tenure.

Taking a company public enables founders and other

members of management who hold unlisted shares, such as myself, to obtain enormous wealth. The company, too, gains access to funds that it can use for purposes such as capital investments. It is no doubt true that there are many executives who would like to take advantage of such benefits.

I felt, however, that in exchange for obtaining such enormous wealth and capital, my ability to manage as I wished would be handicapped—that I would have no choice but to manage in a manner contrary to my philosophy. I resolved, therefore, that instead of being blinded by thoughts of riches, I would be satisfied to have the means to feed myself and to get medical care if I fell ill.

It is only natural for listed companies to emphasize shareholder profits. Looking at recent trends, however, it seems the stock market has been swept by an American-style tendency to prioritize shareholder profit above all. When shareholder profits are a higher priority than employee happiness, there is a tendency to emphasize shareholder dividends over employee salaries. Downsizing is probably the most conspicuous example, and the announcement of restructuring measures often brings an increase in the share price. Steps like these are nothing but an effort to protect the profits of shareholders and investors at the expense of employees.

When I talked to those involved in the stock exchange, or with investors, none of them mentioned anything about employee happiness. Instead, they spoke of the need to release the nearest-term management numbers possible for the sake of evaluating the stock. Settling accounts quarterly is a given, but they also spoke of closing accounts monthly or even daily.

I believe settling accounts once every three years is about right. The reason is that having that much leeway makes it much easier to practice management that takes the long view. Shareholders are supposed to purchase a company's shares because they believe in the company's principles and attitude and want to lend their support. Buying stock out of the expectation that it will rise in value, or intending to sell as soon as it goes up, is just playing games with money.

The stock market today is immature and rampant with such money games. At the extreme, money games create situations in which it is imperative that employee happiness be sacrificed. What is the point of managing a company in such a way? I think this is completely backward, which is why I gave up the idea of going public.

Recently, companies that make a contribution to the global economy have come to be evaluated highly in the stock market. Yet investments in making things more pleasant or enjoyable for employees or in things that are useful to the local community are still not assessed very highly. The perception is that any money invested in such things would be better retained as profit.

There is little hope of managing the way I want under such conditions: managing in a way that gradually increases not sales or profits but employee happiness, and aims for slow growth through tree-ring management. We will put off going public until such time as this kind of approach is appreciated.

Among the people running start-ups today are some who aim from the outset to reap "founder's profits" by becoming listed or going public. They probably think of their companies as tools for making money. Securities firms, it seems, are satisfied to make a good business from dealing with such companies.

And yet, companies have a social responsibility. They must make their employees happy and contribute to society. I sincerely hope that more and more stockholders, analysts, and investors will correctly come to value this kind of approach and take a long-term view in watching over companies.

Good Products Are Not Born of Market Research
When managing in a way that takes the long view, it

becomes critical to sow seeds for the future. For manufacturers like us, that necessitates the research and development of new technologies and new products. At Ina
Foods, more than 10% of our employees are assigned to
our R&D division. In the past, we placed our R&D division on the second floor of our headquarters to show its
importance to the company as a whole.

The space gradually became inadequate, however, so to
commemorate the 50th anniversary of our founding, we
constructed a new, five-story R&D center on a slightly
elevated section of the grounds surrounding our headquarters. This provides considerably more space than we
need given current staffing levels, but we made it spa-
cious, taking future growth into account.

Defining our company as striving for an emphasis on
research and development leads to higher employee motivation. Adopting the approach of contributing to society by creating new products and technologies gives the
impression of a bright and boundless future. I believe
that the management approach of capturing market
share by creating new products that pioneer new markets gives employees much more to look forward to than
engaging in a cutthroat battle of capturing and losing
share in existing markets.

For a product like kanten, for which there was no

existing market in the beginning, we had no choice but to create demand on our own. This is slow work that takes a great deal of persistence, but is also very rewarding.

Our methods of research and development may seem unusual, though. The primary reason is that we do very little market research, something that companies are generally very meticulous about. We do not do any market surveys to determine changes in consumer tastes or to try and find out what is selling best at supermarkets. Neither do we set out to create entirely new product categories that cannot already be found on supermarket shelves. I encourage our people to make products that we ourselves think are good—using our own technology, of course.

I want to stick to our approach of making products that we think are good regardless of whether or not such products already exist or are selling well out in the world. Naturally, we produce some products that do not live up to expectations. Strangely enough, however, this does not bother us very much. The way I see it, we have always worked patiently over time to develop markets from scratch, so our experience gives us the confidence to know that if a product is really good, it will find its place eventually.

Market research is inevitably an investigation of what is already past. The results of this type of research lend themselves to being expressed in numbers, but the numbers themselves are already things of the past. Those who chase numbers are not looking to the future. This is no way to produce good products.

Good products are those that conjure a sense that they will be of use to people, that they will bring people happiness. This might be somewhat difficult to grasp, but I believe good products are those that look to the way people really ought to be—those that follow the direction of human progress.

Products like that are sure to blossom eventually. When a company is impatient, it inevitably rushes to meet short-term needs and tries to come up with products that will sell right away. Why does this happen? Because of its failure to sow seeds in the past. A company that is continually sowing seeds through research and development will always have some flowers blooming.

There are companies that cut back drastically on research and development in times of recession, but I think this has the effect of lowering the morale of employees who become unable to hold onto hope for a brighter future.

Management Should Keep an Eye on Both Progress and Trends

When drawing up a management strategy, I make up my mind based on two coordinate axes: progress and trends.

The progress axis indicates the course of human progress from the past to the present and on to the future. Despite the many twists and turns along the way, in the great flow of things, mankind has made progress in seeking to approach "happiness" and "the ideal." The course of the world's efforts to become a better place and people's efforts to try and become what they are meant to become are plotted along the progress axis. It is, therefore, a time axis extending vertically from the past to the future.

The trend axis indicates the fashions of the day. Think of it as intersecting the progress axis at a right angle and plotting what is popular from one age to the next. Fashions swing like a pendulum, so what interests the world moves back and forth along the trend axis.

When developing new products, for example, it is important to be conscious of both the progress axis and the trend axis. Trends are important, but chasing after them too much can hurt you when the pendulum swings back later on. Instead, we have always tried to take our time in cultivating products aligned with the progress axis. Products that take things in the direction of human happiness will be rewarded eventually.

For instance, there has been a recent trend for "earth-friendly products." Because these seem like the product of fashion, it is tempting to think of them as falling along the trend axis, but since they are rooted in the proposition of human happiness over the long term, this category of products can also be seen as a good fit for the progress axis. Among such products, those that stay on course with the "earth-friendly" progress axis while also riding the trend axis of the day are sure to become hits.

We took a progress-axis approach in developing products under the Kanten Papa brand, adopting the concept of "semi-homemade foods." In a world with more and more families with two working parents, it would have been easy to follow the trend axis with instant food products. On the other hand, amid these same societal changes, homemade foods—the very symbol of a happy family—also provided an opportunity to recapture the way a household ought to be.

We particularly wanted to create products that enabled the whole family, including the father, to enjoy making something together. This follows the progress axis. It also led to the name Kanten Papa. In this way, the Kanten

Papa brand was developed to be firmly grounded in a progress axis perspective, even while being seasoned with a dash of the trend axis.

I am confident that the edible film we have recently developed also follows the progress axis. We developed this transparent kanten film as a way to reduce the use of plastic wrappers and other waste, and already use it to make the inner pouches for our Kanten Soup products. Since the inner pouch is made of edible film, it can simply be dropped in hot water as is. Using such film raises the unit cost by a cent or two compared to conventional pouches, but we think it has the future potential to be used for the inner pouches that come with instant ramen.

One well-known fermented bean product now comes with a special thick sauce incorporating a kanten product that we developed. Previously, eating fermented beans required a separate plastic packet of sauce, but the kanten-based product takes the form of a soft jelly, so it can be mixed in directly. The user's fingers do not get sticky, and the absence of a plastic packet means less waste. I think this is probably another product that can be said to follow the progress axis.

Products that follow only the trend axis may do well for a time, but they fade away quickly and disappear.

Over the long term, such products are inefficient. It really is important, after all, to keep an eye on the progress axis when developing products.

The same thing applies not only to product development but also to drawing up a management strategy. The important thing, I think, is first to look carefully at whether the strategy is a good fit for the progress axis and then to think about how to get on board the trend axis.

Do Not Expand Overseas Just for Cheap Labor

Ina Foods currently has partner factories in four countries: Korea, Chile, Morocco, and Indonesia. We import powdered kanten from these factories as a semi-finished good and then process it in Japan to make our final products. There was a time when we directly imported the seaweed from which kanten is made, but as the technical capability of our partner companies grew, they expressed an interest in expanding their business, so we adopted the system we have today.

We began looking overseas to source our raw ingredients back in the late 1970s. Over the course of Japan's rapid industrial growth, the country's oceans had become quite polluted. Over time, it became harder and harder to secure sufficient high-quality seaweed to make our kanten.

Then we were hit by the oil shock of 1973. The price of kanten skyrocketed and we ended up inconveniencing our trading partners. Feeling this would not do, I traveled the world in search of sources of the seaweed we needed. I went to Australia, Brazil, Mexico, Vietnam, and even as far away as the Azores Islands in the middle of the Atlantic. Our overseas trading began with a search for seaweed suppliers, but meeting people we could trust eventually led to our providing technical assistance and training for the launch of kanten production factories.

As a result, we gained the partner factories that we have today. We have not invested capital in these partner factories. (The one exception is the factory in Chile, which asked us to provide a "friendship investment.") From the outset, we have never exerted control over the local companies by providing such investments. None of our people sit on their boards. Indeed, we do not even send liaison staff.

Although we occasionally send some of our people to provide technical guidance, such business trips only last a couple of weeks. The reason we do not send liaison staff is that I would not want to be posted overseas and I prefer not to ask my employees to do things I would not want to do myself.

Even without making capital investments or sending liaison staff, our relationships with our overseas partner factories are good. This is because from the outset, we did not expand overseas only to make money for ourselves, but rather to prosper together with our partners. Looking at how Japanese companies conduct themselves these days, they often seem to head overseas hoping to take advantage of cheap materials and cheap labor. This is no way to build true relationships of trust.

Chile was the first country from which we imported raw materials. I started out by teaching them step by step what needed to be done: telling them that the seaweed needed to be washed, demonstrating how to sort it, and showing them how it should be dried. Once the sorting and processing operations had improved, we arranged to purchase the product at correspondingly higher prices. The Chileans were thrilled and poured their energy into their washing, sorting, and drying. We had implemented the develop-and-import formula.

We later partnered with a trusted kanten manufacturer to help them make improvements to their kanten factory, agreeing that its products could be sold not only to our company but also in Europe and the United States. Needless to say, that factory has grown smoothly since then.

In Indonesia, we began by providing instruction in

how to farm seaweed, which our company then purchased once it was grown. Today, there is a large kanten production factory there, and kanten has become a major industry in Indonesia. I even received a commendation from Indonesia's Minister of Marine Affairs and Fisheries for our contribution to a national enterprise.

Conditions in Morocco and Korea were different, but in both cases, we followed the develop-and-import formula based on relationships of trust with local people. We pursued our business in a way that took the other party's position into account and tried to ensure that the other party grew. When they produced a better product, we bought it from them at a higher price. When they made quality products after we had given them all the technical guidance we could, we permitted them to sell to others as well. These steps are perfectly natural, yet are not easily taken by a company that thinks only of itself.

Before we knew it, thinking earnestly about the other parties and working together with them over a long period led to the development of relationships of deep trust. Today, even without a contract, they will make whatever we need and provide it just the way we want it. Employees on both sides go back and forth a few times a year, but these visits do not involve difficult business negotiations, and people seem to approach them more like vacations.

CHAPTER 3

Start With the Little Things You Can Do

Take the Long View, But Start with What You Can Do Now

People often say, "Gosh, it's amazing how you were able to keep sales and profits rising for 48 years. What's your secret?" I am frequently asked to give speeches, too, but I usually turn down such offers. The truth is that there is no quick remedy for management. All I can suggest is to "Do what makes sense, as a matter of course," and this does not make for much of a speech.

Managers today spend too much time looking for quick remedies. They spend their time searching for some self-serving way to stand out from the crowd and make a handsome profit. They are probably struggling with the recession, and I can understand where they are coming from, but there is no such thing as a quick fix.

No matter how far it spreads its branches and leaves, a tree whose trunk is weak will fall. It is the same with a company. A company's management philosophy is its trunk, and it must be nurtured without changing. When the going gets tough, there is a tendency to want to change tactics, but any effort that run counter to a company's principles is sure to fail.

In the end, all you can do is take the long view and be persistent in your efforts. But even if you have taken the long view and have a vision for the kind of company you want to become, you still will not get there right away. I think the important thing is to find something you can do right now to prepare, then put it into practice.

Even long-established companies that have been around for hundreds of years did not start out that way. Such companies appear as they do today only because they cherished their founding aims and worked diligently to conduct business the way it was meant to be done.

There are any number of things that small and medium-sized enterprises can do right away. Improving the manner in which employees speak, taking care to greet people politely, or being thorough about cleaning up, for example, are all things that can surely be done immediately and do not cost a thing.

You must not make the mistake of trivializing such things. These are the practices that encourage people to become fans of your company. At Ina Foods, every employee puts all three of these things into practice. Today, everyone is capable of doing so naturally without anyone needing to say a thing.

Neglecting the little things is the same as neglecting the big things. An accumulation of little mistakes becomes a big mistake. Conversely, doing the little things right creates virtuous cycles. When things improve even a little bit, it is human nature to think about how to make them even better still. When all employees are trying to make things a little bit better, a company improves by leaps and bounds.

This is why I speak up even about little things. Every once in a while, someone says, "You're the chairman. You don't need to speak up about such minor details." When this happens, I always ask how they decide what is minor and what is major. Is something major only if a great deal of money is changing hands? Or only if a lot of people are involved? I believe that doing even the small things right is a big deal.

In this sense, managers need to understand what happens even at minor worksites. I often give the example of a single dropped nail. There are people who will carefully pick it up, and people who will let it go as unimportant. But what would happen if that nail punctured the tire of a car traveling on the expressway? It could cause a major accident. You cannot treat even a single nail as something trivial. A single example of a defective product might require you to recall all such products. The little things are important things.

It is meaningless to develop great plans if they go unexecuted. Indeed, it is much more meaningful to find something you can do right now and to start doing it. Even with grand dreams, you have to start with the little things.

The Essence of Management Is Creating Fans

What is the smallest core element for a company? For someone like me who believes that the small things are critical, this is an important question. Elemental particles are the wellspring of all creation, but the elemental particles of a company are what interests me.

I believe the elemental particles of our company are its fans—not its customers, its fans—those people who sincerely support our company's products. I came to the conclusion that in aggregate, these fans form the core of our company.

You could say that creating fans is the essence of corporate management. A manager has to devote a lot of energy to thinking about how to increase the number of people who are fans of his company. Those who purchase our products after seeing mass media advertisements are certainly important customers, but they are not yet fans. Management is all about making the effort to get them to take a step closer and become fans. And this applies not only to customers; I want our suppliers and our business customers and members of the local community to become our fans, too.

Ina Foods reached a milestone in 2008, celebrating the 50th anniversary of its founding. We commemorated the occasion with a garden party, to which we invited about 2,000 people from all over, whom we wanted to thank. To express our gratitude, all 400 of our employees came out to help welcome our guests with homemade cooking. I decided against giving any formal speech, instead choosing to say a word of thanks directly to those who came. Before I knew it, I found I had been standing at the reception line for five hours, saying thanks and shaking hands with people as they arrived.

This year, we also made a contribution to the community by donating funds to the local government for use in promoting our area as a location for shooting the NHK Taiga Drama, an annual, year-long, historical fiction television series.

Wanting also to convey our gratitude to our mail-order customers, we decided to randomly invite 100 of them—50 groups of two—to our headquarters. We took care of hotels and meals and showed them around our company and gardens. When I had time, I met with the customers who came to see us, briefly visiting with them in my office. This sort of event helps develop fans. One customer who visited from Shimane prefecture, for example, later sent me a gift of freshly-harvested rice that he and his wife had grown.

I feel that inviting these customers to visit and learn more about our company, and thereby developing face-to-face relationships with them, helped turn them into true fans. Such fans are added one by one, of course, which probably seems terribly inefficient. It might appear that advertising on television and in newspapers and magazines would be faster. But I believe the opposite is true.

No matter how big one's business is, it ultimately comes down to people dealing with people. If a company is unable to take proper care of each of them, it is sure to decline eventually. If you can treat each and every customer well and turn them all into fans, these new fans will then tell the people around them about your company. This is vastly more effective than mass media advertising. Broadening one's fan base through such viral means is a much better way to increase a company's "elemental particles."

A company's fate lies in how many fans each and every one of its employees can create every day. And it is important to ensure that such efforts are constantly maintained. And isn't it more fun, too, to think of your job as fan creation? Wouldn't it be more exciting to wake up each morning and think about how many fans you could make that day? I think these are precious sentiments.

In order to create fans, you need to make good

products. You must also win the loyalty of both suppliers and customers. It is important, too, to improve the company's image. These are the reasons why we at Ina Foods value our relationships of trust with trading partners, always keep our offices, factories, and gardens looking neat and tidy, and are careful to greet people and watch our choice of words.

Cleaning Is a Silent Salesman

Something that any small or medium-sized enterprise, or even a sole proprietorship, can do right away, and which is unrivaled in its effectiveness (although admittedly when seen over a somewhat longer term) is cleaning. You must not look down on this as "merely cleaning." Cleaning is the secret to business prosperity.

People gather in places that are clean and beautiful. When people come together, value is generated. A company that is thoroughly clean and plants trees and flowers on its grounds improves its image just like that. Surely this is the very foundation of business.

I like to talk about cleaning as a "silent salesman." A clean administrative building or office and carefully tended grounds give customers who visit a sense of security.

But is it enough to hire a cleaning company to clean

things up? No. It is important that employees do the cleaning with their own hands, because this results in something more than simply a clean place: an expression of the company's ideals and philosophy.

The employees of a company that is kept clean speak politely and are quick to smile. Not only are the facilities clean, the people themselves are clean, too. The act of cleaning also polishes the person who does the cleaning. People who visit such a company may feel not only a sense of security but also find themselves deeply impressed. They can feel the presence of management extending into every corner of the organization. Cleaning is truly the best of salesmen.

Let me share one episode that really happened. It relates to one of Kyoto's best-known Japanese confectioners, a long-standing shop with a well-established reputation, the sort of place that does not easily enter into business arrangements with newcomers. Our Osaka sales office approached the company prepared for a long courtship, and it would be misleading to say they gave a warm welcome to a newcomer like our company. I thought this was perfectly understandable.

The president of that confectioner then visited our company while on a package tour. By that time, Kanten Papa Gardens had already become something of a tourist destination drawing 350,000 visitors a year. I suspect he had no special reason to visit, but only came because we were included as a stop on the tour. It seems, though, that he was quite surprised by our well-tended gardens and the cleanliness of our buildings. Immediately after he returned to Kyoto, our Osaka sales office received a call inviting us to visit, and eventually we entered into a business arrangement.

If you clean up only for special occasions, your guests will easily see through it. A company as a whole, as well as its employees, only leaves an impression of cleanliness when it does the cleaning day after day in the same way. The act of cleaning leads people to notice things and nurtures both a sense of belonging and company loyalty.

You probably have occasion to visit various companies from time to time. When you do, it can be useful to observe whether things are kept clean. A company that keeps things clean is one you can trust.

Whenever I hear people say things like "Even the bathroom was clean at that company," or "Who could imagine such a famous company would be so filthy?" or "Seeing how dirty things were there made me a bit worried," it reminds me that people really do have reservations about companies that are not well cleaned.

It is not uncommon to see companies that only clean

the areas people will see, while the back-of-house areas remain dirty. I am unimpressed by companies that engage in such duplicity. It is as if they are publicizing the fact that they are always deceiving people. Such a situation is the worst possible salesman.

Employees at our company keep things clean of their own volition, so they have developed a critical eye for cleanliness. This also means that they have developed a critical eye for their company, for other employees, and for management. Surely it goes without saying how useful this in pursuing our business.

In Our Company Bathrooms, There Is Not a Drop on the Floor

In the bathrooms at Ina Foods headquarters, there is no sign of even a single drop of urine having hit the floor during the 18 years since it was constructed. Of course, achieving a bathroom with no drops on the floor takes more than just appealing to people's idealism and asking them to keep things clean. You also need to address technical questions.

Why do droplets leave the urinal, anyway? Because people stand back from the urinal as they relieve themselves. Why do they stand back? Because they think they will get dirty if they come into contact with the urinal.

If the urinals were clean enough to touch, people would not mind moving closer when relieving themselves. If they did not have to worry about their clothing being soiled through contact with the urinal, they would have the confidence to take a step forward.

In short, if you keep the urinals spotlessly clean, you can prevent even a single drop from leaving them. At our company, employees clean the toilets every day with their bare hands, wiping down both the inside and outside of the bowls, so they are extremely clean. There is no concern about contact, even if you press your trousers against one, so no drops ever hit the floor.

Even if a visitor makes a mistake and drops do end up outside the urinal, employees are in the habit of wiping them up immediately. Whoever notices first just quickly cleans things up. They can do so because they make it a practice to clean the toilets daily. If we were to retain a cleaning company and entrust cleaning the bathrooms to them, our employees would probably stop wiping things up themselves.

Not just bathrooms, but any place that is kept clean is less likely to become dirty. And anyone who does get it dirty wants to make it clean again right away. Surely this is human nature.

Occasionally, I see areas along the road where litter

that people have discarded has accumulated. Left unaddressed, such areas simply attract more and more garbage. Posting signs that say "No Littering" has no effect. But I hear that if flowers are planted in such places, the littering stops. Clean places get cleaner, while dirty places just get dirtier and dirtier.

I constantly tell our employees that if we ever reach the point where we cannot keep things clean, then our company will fail. If I run across a spot that has not been properly cleaned, I make a point to mutter, "Our company is going downhill." And I mean it, too.

Diligently working to keep things clean demonstrates a level of attachment to the company. The act of cleaning engenders feelings of attachment, and feelings of attachment make one want to keep things clean. I think that is just the way it is.

What about an office that is clean and neat and decorated with flowers? Isn't that enough to stir people's motivation all by itself? And it is not just offices. Keeping the equipment clean in the factories improves uptime and reduces employee injuries. Cleaning the equipment engenders feelings of attachment, and feelings of attachment lead to even better maintenance, fostering the kind of advantages that are not listed in equipment catalogs.

Most of all, though, cleaning improves the workplace

environment and makes things more pleasant for the people who work there. It is directly related to our company's management objective of increasing employee happiness.

In order for employees to be able to go about cleaning more pleasantly and enjoyably, management cannot be stingy about making efforts to provide the proper tools and making sufficient time available. At our company, we have a tool shed on site, equipped with brooms, shovels, weed-whackers, lawn mowers, leaf blowers, sickles, pruning shears, and every other kind of tool needed to maintain the gardens. These tools are made freely available for employees to use not only at the company but also at home if they wish.

People often say we can do such things only because we have resources to spare, but that is not the case at all. Even when we had nothing, we made it a point to keep things clean.

Create Small Things to Look Forward to an Increase in Employee Motivation

When I joined Ina Foods, the company was struggling from a lack of funds. Even if we wanted to equip ourselves with proper production machinery, there was no money to buy it with. We had no choice but to put our heads together to find ways to streamline and raise productivity. That is why, even now I think it is important to find ways to improve production and management efficiency without spending money.

If you mention raising productivity with managers today, they immediately think about purchasing new equipment and adopting IT solutions. Certainly, efforts at mechanization, energy efficiency, and computerization are important. But these efforts only really bear fruit when paired with on-site ingenuity. The first thing to do is to get all employees to put their heads together. Their wisdom is boundless. Whenever I see someone obsessed only with buying something new, I cannot help telling him to knock it off.

You can never achieve true efficiency and streamlining as long as you rely on machines or equipment. You must look to more fundamental measures—how to raise people's motivation. There is no better policy for improved efficiency and streaming than raising employee motivation.

People who are motivated, physically active, and sharing ideas can double or triple what they are capable of. This is much more efficient than increasing equipment uptime or purchasing new machines. If the 480 employees at our company could all work twice as effectively, it would be like having 960 employees. Productivity would increase dramatically.

Having gone through a period of scarcity, I became convinced that the greatest policy for raising productivity is raising employee motivation. Raising employee motivation is much more powerful than introducing new machines or IT, although many managers seem confused on this point. As I constantly say, what raises employee motivation is the real sense that they are happier this year than last year, and will be even happier next year than this year.

For a while after Ina Foods was established, however, we certainly did not have the resources to make anyone feel that way at all. I thought long and hard back then about how to come up with something for everyone to look forward to that would raise employee motivation.

At the time, we were constantly building and expanding our facilities. Everyone worked overtime late into the night, not only producing kanten, but also doing things like laying concrete floors and setting water tanks in place. After finishing work for the day, we always went out for a drink together. Looking back on this now, it was only a small thing to look forward to, but it did raise employee motivation. The employees were able to gird themselves to work hard again the next day.

I also used to set specific goals, and when we met them, everyone would go to a local inn for a banquet. There were times when everyone went straight back to work from the inn the next morning. We managed to enjoy ourselves and raise motivation by setting an objective and feeling the sense of accomplishment that came from meeting it.

All you can expect of machinery is the capabilities written about in the catalogs. But people are different. When motivated to do so, they will start chasing after work themselves. Instead of being pursued by work, they start to pursue work on their own. The difference is enormous. There are no catalog values for human capability; if sufficiently motivated, people are capable of exerting double or triple, and sometimes even five or 10 times their ordinary power.

I believe that managers need to fully understand this and think about ways to motivate their employees before flipping longingly through the pages of high-priced equipment catalogs.

A Company Whose Trips Are Fun Is a Cohesive Company

Since 1969, Ina Foods has held company-sponsored trips overseas every other year. This has continued for nearly 45 years now. When we started, it was unusual for a company to arrange trips overseas. Employees save up some of the funds for these trips on their own, but the company subsidizes them whether the destination is overseas or domestic.

In 2008, to commemorate our 50th anniversary, we raised the budget by 100,000 yen (US $970) per employee to enable each of them to travel to Europe. Those who elected to go to Europe headed off to locations such as Paris, Rome, and Germany. Other employees chose to take tours of New Zealand or Hokkaido. Employees split into 13 separate groups and went on their way.

Company trips play a role in employee welfare, providing recreation and relaxation, but they are also very effective in terms of education. There is a broadening of horizons that comes from visiting foreign lands, and being in a different environment also provides opportunities for re-evaluating oneself.

When traveling in a developing country, for example, it is not uncommon to find that while the hotel in which one is staying is beautiful, there is abject squalor in the alleyways out back. I have heard that some employees who saw such things for themselves realized that they would be embarrassed if their own workplaces and factories were not kept clean, both in the back-of-house areas as well as those visible to outsiders. Similar to the old saying about correcting one's own behavior by observing the faults of others, whether it is with respect to cleaning, greetings, choice of words, or interacting with people, employees always come back having learned a great deal.

Whenever I hear managers grumbling about how their younger employees look displeased when mandatory company trips are discussed, I cannot help thinking what a shame this is. Surely this sort of thing happens because the company's trips are not fun. If company trips are no fun, it means the workplace is no fun. The employees who work in such places are probably unhappy. One could hardly expect such trips to boost their morale.

Fortunately, employees at our company all look forward to our company trips. I believe this is because they are joined together by family-like bonds, so our company trips are really family trips for the "Ina Foods family."

Some members of our team have disabilities. I sometimes worry that this might present challenges for travel, but other employees always reassure me that they will watch out for them, so they come along, too. If employees were thinking only of themselves, they would not make such efforts. Things like this remind me again and again that they really are a family.

When employees get along well, it creates a completely different atmosphere when planning the trips, too. Instead of choosing among the standard packages offered by travel agents, like-minded employees group together and put together their own travel plans. One group that went to New Zealand, for example, traveled more than 500 kilometers by motorcycle and rental car before arriving at their destination.

Taking company trips together brings employees closer together. This makes for a workplace that is more fun and creates a more positive atmosphere, which has a positive effect on their work itself, making it more enjoyable through the generation of virtuous cycles.

In such an atmosphere, when a given employee experiences hardship, everyone else tries to help out. For example, the son of an employee at one of our subsidiaries was involved in an accident in which he fell from his fourth floor apartment. Employees immediately began collecting donations and raised quite a bit of money for the family.

When an employee's home was destroyed in a fire, we sent teams of employees to provide emergency assistance. Donations were collected, of course, and our company issued an interest-free loan to help rebuild the home.

This cohesion between the company and its employees is one of the greatest strengths of Ina Foods.

Be Generous with Investments That Protect Employee Welfare

Ina Foods has endeavored to improve its workplace environment ever since the early years when it struggled financially. I was personally working on the shop floor, doing manual labor such as boiling and pressing seaweed, so I had a very clear picture of the difficulties that workers faced there.

The process of making kanten involves large volumes of water, and there were always puddles of water around everyone's feet. Everything was always wet, so the factory itself felt unclean. Back then, all employees went about their work wearing long rubber boots and heavy rubber aprons. Working under such chilly, wet conditions every day led to some employees developing rheumatism-like symptoms.

To improve conditions in our workplace, I launched the "Sayonara to Rubber Boots" campaign. I wanted to create a workplace where employees could work in sneakers instead of rubber boots.

It would have been easy to get rid of the puddles if we had possessed the funds: all we would have had to do was install receptacles to catch the water where it spilled and then periodically empty them all at once. At the time, though, we had no money, so we put employee creativity and ingenuity to the test in order to reduce leaks and cobbled together our own water receptacles to eliminate puddles. Ultimately, we managed to create an environment conducive to working in sneakers. At the same time, we also instituted the practice of keeping things well cleaned.

There is one other experience from the early days of our company that I cannot forget. At the time, the press we used to remove water when making tokoroten—a kind of thin, sweet jelly noodle—employed heavy weights. One of the weights slipped and struck an employee, who suffered a complex fracture so severe that he was forced to stay away from work for a long time.

I did not dismiss this as a mere accident. Could we really continue exposing our employees to such dangerous conditions in their work? Wasn't our company responsible for the safety of its employees?

To continue using our existing press would leave open the possibility that similar accidents would occur. Buying a new press would solve the problem, but it required substantial funds. The amount was so large that it was really an overinvestment for our company at the time.

It was an investment of such magnitude that it risked shaking the very foundations of the company, to say nothing of recovering the cost. I struggled with the decision. It was only natural to want to ensure employee safety, but all would be for naught if the purchase led to the failure of the company.

Ultimately, after much reflection, I decided to buy the new press. I chose in favor of a safer work environment, deciding that if our company was going to make its employees unsafe, then it would be better for it to disappear.

So what happened after we introduced the new, mind-bogglingly expensive press? First, things were safer. In addition, we also saw a large rise in productivity. But most of all, the employees were thrilled and showed a huge increase in motivation. This all had a positive effect on company operations.

In the end, then, my decision was a great success. I also learned something very important. The good results came from the fact that the motive—a desire to protect employees from harm—was correct. I came to believe that things would work out if the motive was right, and became firmly convinced that I must not skimp on investments that protect employees.

During the kanten boom in 2005, we adopted a

three-shift system for the first time, and ran our factories around the clock. As I previously mentioned, this was something that our employees put into practice voluntarily in order to meet the sudden surge in demand. Inevitably, though, a number of employees fell ill, so we stopped.

There are some managers who think they can get three times as much out of the same factory by implementing a three-shift system, but I disagree. With the exception of industries in which stopping plant operations causes material energy loss, I believe that ordinary businesses should avoid night shift work as much as possible if they care about employee well-being.

Management is a Game of Concentrating Everyone's Power

Board meetings at Ina Foods take the form of what might be called "idle chatter." Except in special cases when there are pressing issues to decide, no particular agenda is set. Each director gives a report on the week, and then everyone talks about the issues that came up.

These reports are not typical business reports, though. Instead, directors may ramble on about what happened during the week, or who visited, or whatever is on their mind. Sometimes we may even talk about news events that have no direct bearing on our company at all.

And yet, all this chatter enables us to share a great deal of fine-grained information. It is one way of trying to make Ina Foods a company with an atmosphere that is as positive and open as possible. Talking together about various events instead of simply reporting numbers leads to much deeper mutual understanding. Even talking over news stories—thinking about what we might do if such and such a thing were to happen, or whether anything could have been done in advance—leads naturally to the development of a consensus among the directors about where our company is going and how it should respond.

As the chairman, I tend to do a lot of the talking, but it is not at all unusual for the directors to ignore what I am saying as side conversations pop up. I do not, after all, insist that everyone listen reverently to what I have to say. People cut me off freely when I am speaking, too, during our animated discussions. Sometimes I even have to say, "Okay, enough already. Be quiet and listen to me for a minute, will you?" Such board meetings are really conversational free-for-alls.

It is important that employees as well as directors are able to talk freely among themselves. A company whose employees listen to their superiors' instructions and then speak ill of them behind their backs has a problem. There are some companies whose directors each have private offices and seem to retreat into their own shells. Why do they need private offices? It only impedes communication.

I know of one company listed on the Tokyo Stock Exchange whose directors work in glassed-in offices—not so much separate rooms as areas separated by glass partitions. The desks they use are the same as those of regular employees. Directors can easily see what the employees are doing and employees can easily see what the directors are doing. I was impressed with this open workplace and the good communication it fosters.

I think of management as a game, one whose goal is to figure out how to raise everyone's sense of solidarity. To use a sports analogy, it is like soccer in the sense that it requires teamwork. The work of a company manager is to concentrate everyone's power—that of directors, employees, part-time workers, and even trading partners—and get it moving in the same direction. If people are dissonant, their power is diminished, but when everyone acts in perfect harmony, the company is able to exert its greatest possible power. An awl punches a hole because it focuses on a single sharp point. It is the same with a company.

What would happen if directors and employees, and each individual among them, all faced in different directions? One plus one would not even equal two. In order to bring together the power of everyone involved with the company, good communication is critical. I welcome small talk and jokes that lighten the mood if they improve communication and help clear the air. This is why I value the spirit of harmony: because it is essential for concentrating people's power.

These days it seems as if more and more companies are introducing work-at-home options as a way of improving efficiency. I think this is a mistake. I am sure workers have their own reasons for preferring such arrangements, but from a company management perspective, they lead to a diffusion of energy.

In the same way, I am also opposed to spinning off companies. Some say that spinning off parts of a company as independent entities raises motivation, but if you think about it rationally, you can see that this only leads to a diffusion of energy. This may be unavoidable at huge companies, but I have decided for myself not to engage in corporate spin-offs.

CHAPTER 4

Managers Must Be Educators

If You Want to Be Happy, Do Something People Will Thank You For

There is something about the state of education today that should raise concerns: neither parents nor schools are engaged in real education. When it comes to real education, things like raising percentile scores and getting into good universities are only secondary concerns; the most important thing is to teach how we should live as human beings—the proper way to live our lives.

People have recently made a great fuss about how the academic ability of Japanese children has fallen relative to other countries. The Ministry of Education, Culture, Sports, Science, and Technology has admitted the failings of its "room to grow" program and changed course back toward more intensive studying. Yet no matter how high test scores may rise, can they really be said to lead to international competitiveness?

I believe the advantage in truly competing internationally is determined by how many of our citizens really have a sense for what is the right thing to do, for how to live their lives. Given how prosperous Japanese society has become, it is not normal that almost 30,000 Japanese people commit suicide every year. I think we have no choice but to admit that there is something wrong with our education system. This is a problem that should come before international competition.

Living happily is the goal of life, a human right and a human responsibility. This is what I believe. People must live even if they are poor, even if they fall ill, even if unpleasant things happen to them. Yet even fundamentals such as these are no longer taught in our schools.

The young employees who come into our company now are meek. In the old days of scarcity, people used to arrive with a well-developed sense of cunning, but I do not see very much of this in young people today. If given proper direction, they can easily be turned onto the correct path. Conversely, if they are taught that profit-making is the proper course, they will become steeped in such thinking.

Takafumi Horie, the entrepreneur popularly known as Horiemon who gained fame as president of Livedoor, is probably a classic example. It seems he aspired to build a company with the largest market capitalization in the world. But this is not a true aspiration, because it lacks the spirit of public service. Indeed, far from thinking of public service, he seemed to feel that it was all right to deceive society for his own gain. Someone like that might graduate from the University of Tokyo but still be useless without the correct mindset. To think solely of oneself, I think, is nothing but naked ambition.

Building a huge company is not the best way for people to find happiness, and neither is making a lot of money. But the gratitude of others is. Doesn't it make you feel really happy when you do something for someone else that they appreciate? Buddhism teaches the concept of altruism, suggesting that if you want to become happy, you should do something for which others will be grateful.

I have been managing a company for more than half a century and I have never lost a thing by helping other people. Indeed, everything I have done for others has returned to me even greater. This is something I can say with conviction based on my experience.

At Kanten Papa Hall, we hold exhibitions of paintings and ceramics. Since we are able to exhibit really wonderful works of art, we do as much as we can to publicize these events, putting up banners on pedestrian overpasses and running advertisements in the newspaper. We do this because we want to build excitement around the exhibitions and ensure they are a success. It costs money, but it also brings joy both to visitors and exhibiting artists. The exhibits also improve the image of our company, and sometimes artists even thank us with gifts of artwork from their exhibits. These are benefits brought about by altruism.

My own pet theory is that companies ought to be educational institutions and managers ought to be educators. Since companies have a great deal of power through their authority over personnel matters, it ought to be easy for them to educate their employees. Properly educating the employees they have hired is also another way of contributing to the community.

Being Upstanding Means Not Creating Trouble for Other People

Believing as I do that managers must be educators, my educational objective is to build "upstanding members of society." Having put it in this way, readers may wonder exactly what I mean by "upstanding."

Does it mean achieving great renown as a politician? Does it mean succeeding in business and earning a great deal of money? Amassing a great fortune? I think it means something else.

When I talk about someone who is "upstanding," I mean someone who does not create trouble for others. Those who create trouble for others are "bad people." Those who do not create trouble for society or for others are "upstanding people." There are, however, three levels of "upstanding."

First there is "somewhat upstanding," which simply

means not causing trouble for others. Second, there is "very upstanding," which means doing at least a little something that is useful to others. That is, it goes beyond merely not causing trouble for others to include also doing something that is good, even if it is very minor. This might, for example, be something useful done for family or friends.

Finally, there is "extremely upstanding," the most upstanding of them all, which means being of use to many people or to society as a whole—doing good things that benefit many people, including strangers who are neither family nor friends. Those who take care to be "extremely upstanding" are sure to receive great happiness in return.

In order to teach the concept of being upstanding to employees, managers are called upon to be upstanding themselves. If managers only talk about being upstanding and fail to act accordingly, employees will simply ignore them. Even if a manager is clever and makes a name for himself, he can hardly be called upstanding if in his shadow there are employees who have been cast aside by downsizing and trading partners driven into bankruptcy. After all, he will have created enormous trouble for them all.

Having defined "upstanding" as not creating trouble

for others, as a manager myself, I have always tried my best to create the least possible trouble for our company, our employees, our trading partners, and all the people with whom we are involved. If this stance resonates with our employees, then I think it will lead our company itself to become upstanding.

The rule about not creating trouble for others is very easy to understand and immediately applicable, whether in the context of managing a company, running a business, or just living in society. It also makes sense to both children and adults.

Although it is only a little thing, I counsel employees at Ina Foods to park their cars in a spot some distance from the building when they shop at supermarkets and the like. This is a matter of taking care to ensure that they do not create even a minor inconvenience for other customers who may have mobility issues and really need the closer spots.

I also prohibit employees who drive to work in their own cars from making right turns onto our company grounds during the morning rush hour. This is because trying to turn right (when driving on the left, as we do in Japan) inevitably leads to traffic congestion while the driver waits for an opening in the cross traffic. Although slightly less convenient for them, I have employees take the long way around and turn left onto the property instead. I doubt local residents have noticed, but this is all part of not causing trouble for others.

The accumulation of such modest gestures has the positive effect of raising the image of our company. Yet not creating trouble for others only meets the minimum standard of "somewhat upstanding." I hope that by seeking to be of use to others we can aim higher, for "very upstanding" or "extremely upstanding."

To do so, it is important to use the skills that we have mastered through experience, not only to benefit ourselves, but also to be useful to others. People grow, and over time they gain wisdom and skills and broaden their personal connections. If a person uses these new strengths to help someone or to make the world a better place, then that person will surely develop into an upstanding person.

Training for New Employees Begins with a Hundred-Year Calendar

Training for new employees at our company is a bit unusual. We put off skill acquisition for later and begin by showing our new employees a hundred-year calendar. A hundred-year calendar, as you might imagine, is a calendar with the next 100 years printed on a single sheet of paper. We have such hundred-year calendars posted here and there around the company, so employees probably run across them a few times a day, and in doing so, undoubtedly renew their sense of resolve.

When I stand before new employees, I say, "Take a good look at this hundred-year calendar, okay? Somewhere on it you will find the date of your death. In my case, it is probably up toward the top. In your case, it is probably somewhere in the middle, but it is undoubtedly there."

New employees are invariably bewildered by this sudden talk of the date of their death. The young do not give much thought to death, which is why they assume they have unlimited time left. Showing them a hundred-year calendar, though, gives them a visceral sense that their own lives are limited.

"Let's put the date of your death in here, then. Think about how you are going to live your life—the only one you have—until then. Imagine you were going to take a trip to Hawaii. If you could only stay a week, you would probably be beside yourself trying to do all sorts of things for fear of wasting even a single minute. Surely none of you would want to spend all day idling away in your hotel room."

I tell them that it is the same with life. No matter how

young you are, your remaining time is limited. Surely you lose out if while you are alive, you do not use your head and your body to do everything that you possibly can. "And if you want to be happy," I tell them, "do something that will make other people happy." What I mean, of course, is that they should adopt the altruistic mindset that I mentioned earlier.

If a hundred-year calendar is hard to grasp, imagine a thousand-year calendar. Both my own date of death and those of younger people would fall in essentially the same place up at the top. In the grand scheme of things, even the lives of those who live the longest are terribly short. Is it really all right to just try and take it easy?

The world today is awash with the notion that anything fun is good, but this is wrong. The more struggle involved in a job, the greater the sense of accomplishment will be when it is done. Nothing makes a person happier than being useful to someone and being appreciated for it. We only have one life, and it would be a terrible loss not to experience such joy and emotion.

During their training, employees also study the 1890 Imperial Rescript on Education. This document was rejected by the democratic post-war educational system, but I believe it describes many important norms that society should follow. It describes aspects of traditional

Japanese morality, such as filial piety, fraternity, conjugal harmony, character building, and the philanthropic spirit. I think people benefit from learning about this document while they are still young.

After two weeks of training, new employees have a completely new outlook. They decide that they want to do everything they possibly can in the limited time they have. Rather than feeling compelled by the company to work, they feel that it would be their own loss not to work as hard as they can.

If employees really come to believe that they are not working to make the company money but rather for their own happiness, they will take action all by themselves. This is why our employees come early to work to clean things up without anyone telling them to do so: because they understand that it is a loss to their own lives if they do not get their minds and bodies moving.

At new employee training, we thoroughly hammer home the notion of the "Five S" methodology: seiri, seiton, seiso, seiketsu, and shitsuke (sort, straighten, shine, standardize, and sustain). Performing any of these actions involves the use of the body. Once employees understand that not moving is a loss to themselves, they start to grasp things even more quickly.

All of these items are perfectly ordinary, yet if people

are incapable of doing even such simple things, then any management strategy, no matter how lofty, is meaningless. The Five S's are fundamental for employees and fundamental for companies.

The Highest Priority When Hiring Is the Ability to Cooperate

My highest priority when hiring employees is their ability to cooperate. No matter how talented or well educated a potential employee might be, I will not hire someone who lacks the ability to cooperate.

Having the ability to cooperate means thinking about others and being open to mutual support. Those who are cooperative can therefore be expected to be highly attentive in their everyday lives. Being sensitive to the needs of others is one example.

Who doesn't feel good when someone offers an energetic "good morning" at the start of the day? It is also important to be able to tell a joke and lighten the mood during downtime. Taking the initiative to clean things up is another example of cooperation.

These sorts of actions, which may at first glance seem unrelated to work, are highly valued at our company. We explain all this to those who arrive seeking positions with us. Some do seem puzzled, but most understand where we are coming from. There are even some who break into tears.

We want those who join our company to understand that the employees of Ina Foods are family. Because we are a family, there is no labor union. There is no need for one. Those whom we choose not to hire receive a hand-written rejection letter from our human resources staff. They applied to work for us, after all, so they surely have feelings of some sort toward our company. Even though we were unable to hire them, we send such letters in the hope that they will still become fans of our company.

Very few people choose to leave our company mid-career, and part-time workers often become regular employees. The door is open to those who have drive and talent in the broad sense, along with cooperation skills, to be promoted to regular employees. Those who are promoted in this way are thrilled that such a thing should happen to a "lowly part-timer," and apply themselves even more diligently to their work. Seeing this, other regular employees and new hires are also motivated to work harder. This is another example of a virtuous cycle.

When hiring, we do not ask about academic background, but we do administer a simple test of common knowledge, something like, "Draw a map of Japan."

People have surprising difficulty doing so. Why do applicants have a hard time drawing a map of Japan when they surely see one every day in the weather report? I think this shows the measure of their awareness of issues and their attention to detail.

Knowledge gained by studying at a desk is of little use in actual work. Knowledge is nothing more than knowledge; what is required is wisdom. Wisdom is knowledge plus experience. Wisdom is not generated unless both knowledge and experience are in harmony. And even when sharing the same experience, those who are attentive will gain greater wisdom. This is why paying attention is so important.

When I evaluate people, I try to look not at ability, but at effort. Rather than considering differences in ability, I examine how much effort they put into making use of the abilities they have.

The results- and ability-oriented approach taken by most of the world today does not really look at ability; it assesses only results. Effort is given no consideration at all. Such a context does not foster a desire to encourage others to do their best or think of the company as a whole and does nothing to raise either cooperation or attention, no matter how much time passes. I cannot imagine that such companies will be able to endure.

Posted on the wall at our company's research and development division is a sign that reads, "Serendipity," a word reflecting the division's knack for discovering things by chance that they were not looking for at all. I treasure this word because it really captures the essence of our research capabilities.

This knack for the serendipitous is something I want all of our employees to have, not just those in R&D. If every employee were able to take advantage of serendipity, our company would be a mountain of treasures. Serendipity comes into play when people are attentive to those around them and notice the small things.

Compliance Is a Given, Not a Goal

In the last 10 years, there has been a great deal of annoying talk about "compliance." I find it incredibly strange that there is any need to go out of one's way to emphasize compliance. Surely following the law is something we can be expected to do as a matter of course, without being told. To see leading companies touting "compliance" as one of their corporate principles leaves me speechless. That they feel they must go out of their way to emphasize compliance suggests the depths of the dysfunction in today's corporate society.

To be perfectly clear, I can't stand the word "compliance."

One reason is that I feel there should be no reason at all to even mention such an ordinary thing. Another reason is that the word has taken on a life of its own, as if every little thing needs to be done strictly according the letter of the law.

Laws are made to serve some objective. There is nothing good about a world in which this is forgotten, where people are disciplined only because they infringe on the written provisions of the law. Laws offer nothing more than benchmarks and standards. Laws come alive in the real world only when given some leeway for application and interpretation on a case-by-case basis. Applying them inflexibly leads to behaviors that do not serve society and are done only to conform to the law.

Here is an example that took place within our company. A public road designated as a wide-area agricultural road passes through the center of the Ina Foods grounds. When the road was being widened, the planned sidewalk portion would have overlapped with a number of big pine trees that had been on the site for a long time. The city office said that regulations called for them to be cut down, but I put a stop to it. I thought they should be left standing both from a scenic and an environmental perspective, and there was plenty of space available for the sidewalk even if the pines were left as they were. The city office said that regulations were regulations, and if they were not followed, the work would be ineligible to receive government subsidies. I pushed back and negotiated to put up the money instead.

Similarly, when we sought to plant cherry trees along one embankment, we ended up having to suspend our plans. As it turned out, the embankment was the property of the national government, and apparently it was forbidden to plant anything there without the government's permission. Although it would have been better for both the scenery and the environment, things did not go as we wished because we were bound by the law.

What was really aggravating, though, was what happened when employees at one of our branches cleaned the bathrooms at a nearby park. The city office told them that if they were to clean the bathrooms, it would cause others to lose their jobs. Our employees felt that they had no choice but to back down but decided that they could plant flowers in the park instead. This time, they were told that they needed official permission to do so. What in the world is the point of regulations that get in the way of virtuous behavior?

There are even more examples. Within Kanten Papa Gardens, there are two spots where it is possible to draw delicious water from an underground well. People in the local area are free to bring plastic containers and fill them from these wells. We thought about using this water in the on-site restaurants, but under current laws, it seems we cannot do so without sterilizing it first. What sense does it make to insist that delicious natural water be tainted by chlorination?

Laws, ordinances, and regulations exist to make people happy. Of course there are bad people, and there is certainly a need to keep crime under control, but something is wrong when even virtuous actions are not permitted.

For example, imagine there is a pond and placed in front of it is a sign that says, "No Swimming Allowed." What would you do if a child were drowning in the pond? Would it be correct to follow the sign and just watch? Of course not. The right thing to do would be to jump in and save the drowning child.

I feel tremendous dissatisfaction and anxiety about the tendency to explain away everything with the word "compliance." I believe it is important that the citizenry become conscious of the fact that what leads directly to human happiness is correct, above and beyond the law.

Adversity Builds Character
People grow through adversity. In my case, I was raised

in poverty. Born in 1937, I was eight years old when the war ended. That same year, my father, who was a Western-style painter, passed away at the young age of 40. My mother raised the five children he left behind all by herself.

My mother often said to me, "When you grow up, please don't be an artist like your father. I want you to be able to live a normal life." Since my mother had to work, I took responsibility for all the housework while I was still in elementary school. I often had to miss classes as a result, and sometimes I would go to school, return home in the middle of the day to do housework, and then head off to school again. I can remember tilling our tiny garden with my younger brother during the early years after the war, when food was scarce.

I managed to graduate from middle school and was able to attend high school while working part-time. As I previously mentioned, however, I came down with pulmonary tuberculosis as a result of overwork and malnourishment, and was forced to drop out. In the depths of poverty, I was afflicted by a disease that could have ended my life. I had many heartbreaking and difficult days then, but it was not all bad. The adversity I faced then laid the foundation for the person I would become. Poverty, heartbreak, hardship, and sadness all cultivate a person's character.

Experiencing terrible adversity in my own life has enabled me to understand the pain and hardship of others. I know full well the power of human kindness and the importance of having hope, no matter how small. This is not a matter of reason, but something you can only grasp through experience.

Thanks to my own experience of poverty and illness as a boy, I developed a strong determination to manage in a way that takes care of people. For a while after it was founded, Ina Foods was a poor company. Even then, I worked hard to take care of my comrades and avoid causing trouble for our trading partners. I was determined that even when the pressure begin to ease, I would not act selfishly and desert either our employees or those who had helped us in the past.

When I recovered from pulmonary tuberculosis, I swore to myself that I would have no need for luxury and would simply live as industriously as I could. After joining Ina Foods, I worked for 10 or more hours every day, with no weekends off. This was not hardship, because I was happy just to be able to work.

The world is full of excess now, and there is far less material hardship than before. This is why it is necessary that young people be proactive in seeking to shoulder hardship for themselves. The experience of seeking out difficulty and overcoming adversity is certain to make them bigger, stronger people.

Young people today seem to always try to choose the easiest path, as if it were to their advantage to do so. Even after joining a company, they think about finding an easier job with higher pay, and as soon as they find one, they jump ship.

One young person told me, "Those who cling to a company where they cannot achieve self-actualization are losers," but people who say this sort of thing are exactly the kind of people who will never be able to achieve self-actualization.

I look for people who are determined to work hard and change the company for the better, to make the company a place where self-actualization is possible. The people who take this attitude and work hard will wake up one day and find themselves directors.

Those who exert little effort themselves but are quick to complain and blame their companies do not yet have a solid foundation as individuals. I felt my life would be miserable if it ended in poverty, and I worked hard to change my life by myself. I wish more young people had the backbone to try and change things for themselves.

The Measure of a Company's Value Is Its Level of Employee Happiness

I think our society needs a radical change of values as we look to the future. In the corporate world, too, we need a new measure to replace conventional rankings by sales volume and profitability. As I have said throughout this book, I believe that a company exists to make its employees happy and to contribute to society by doing so.

Therefore, I've been thinking hard about whether there is a way to use employee happiness as an alternative measure of a company's value. At the very least, I have used employee happiness as a guide, if a somewhat fuzzy one, in my own management.

Thinking along these lines, one wonders whether it is enough for only employees to be happy. What about the people at our subcontractor companies, or those working for our trading partners, or our customers? We could expand even further to ask about Japanese society as a whole, or even the entire world.

To put this in simple terms, even if you are managing a profitable company, you can hardly say you are creating happiness if, at the end of the day, you have members of the working poor among your extended family. If Japan develops alone, without making a contribution to the world, it will eventually wind up being rejected by everyone else. Recently, it has become more and more important to make a contribution to the global environment.

There are limits to what any one company can do, and this is certainly the case with small and medium-sized enterprises such as ours. But even though we are small, I want us to be moving in the right direction. Many small entities gathered together are sure to generate enormous power.

For example, many Japanese companies have established production bases in China. I am sure this has led to increased sales for these companies, and profits, too. And yet shifting production to China has put people in Japan out of work. This certainly will not lead to a prosperous community.

There has been an increase in inexpensive imported goods in Japan. This may seem at first to be advantageous for consumers, but is it really? The rise of imports has also led to a decline in prices for conventional products. That is, there has been a decline in added value to the Japanese economy. Japan today is seeing a rapid drop in added value, and neither companies nor employees can prosper under such conditions. I really wish someone would research trends in added value in Japan over time.

So what should Japan do going forward?

One possible solution I see is to make tourism a priority, that is, to make the shift from manufacturing superpower to tourism superpower. I think this is probably one direction Japan could take to survive going forward.

This way of thinking is why we have been pouring our energy into the development of Kanten Papa Gardens. In the beginning, we never could have imagined that a kanten manufacturer in rural Nagano prefecture would one day draw 350,000 tourists a year. Yet after 30 years of improving the gardens little by little, all of the sudden we find ourselves here.

Today Kanten Papa Gardens has come to play a major role in establishing a positive image of our company. Visitors who come to our grounds become fans of the company and purchase our products. In the same way, I am sure that if tourists visiting Japan decide they like the country, they will purchase Japanese products, too. This is what I mean by suggesting that Japan make tourism a priority.

There are five essential elements needed in order to create this kind of tourism. First, you have to have something worth seeing. Second, buying must be a pleasant experience. Third, you have to offer delicious things to eat. Fourth, visitors need to be able to learn something.

Fifth, the experience needs to be relaxing.

When all five elements are in place, the stage is set for successful tourism. If companies all around Japan aspire to create such tourism opportunities, Japan will surely become a tremendous tourist destination.

Aim to Innovate in Order to Keep Doing the Ordinary

Carrying on with the ordinary—continuity—is important. Many people have made this argument, and I have already mentioned that I feel the same way. However, it is important not to mistake continuity for always doing the same thing. If you just keep doing the same thing, nothing will last.

Our company trips have continued for 45 years, but if we always took the same trip, the program would surely not have lasted. It is only because we try something new every year that employees enjoy these trips and want them to continue. Even with our morning meetings and daily exercises, we are always innovating. We put our heads together and try to find ways to make things even better. If we didn't, such things would not continue.

Trying to ensure that a company endures works the same way. In order for a company to endure, it must continually innovate. We try to ensure that waves of innovation are constantly sweeping across every division, through the introduction of new management techniques, new products, new technologies, and new services.

When I look at our directors and our employees, I can see that some are better than others at carrying out continual innovation. To some degree, I think this may be a matter of personal disposition. Yet at any company, no matter how small, top management must always be aiming for innovation. The most important thing when nurturing successors is surely to ingrain in them the habit of innovation.

It is all right to begin with something small. You could vary the layout of table and chairs depending on the content of the meeting, or change the position of your desk, or change the flowers, or the pictures hanging on the wall. These are the sorts of things I think anyone could start with.

Some readers may scoff and wonder what impact such things could possibly have, but getting in the habit of questioning why things have to be in a certain place will serve you well in your work. Asking "Why?" is the first step toward innovating.

When wooden clogs were replaced with shoes, the craftsmen who made clogs had a difficult time becoming shoemakers, so stores that sold clogs rarely became shoe stores. Even within the footwear business, it was not easy to transition smoothly from one technique to another.

If you give up and decide that clogs and shoes are completely different, it's all over. But surely the people involved in making clogs would have been better suited for work in shoes than people with no knowledge of footwear or the human foot. The transition from the clog business to the shoe business really ought to be one of the great case studies in innovation in response to changing times. I think the reason it did not work out this way was that they were unable to distinguish between what needed to be changed and what could not be changed. What they needed to change was their product, and what could not be changed was the business approach of providing people with comfortable footwear.

Although a company's products and services may change to fit the times, it must not change its fundamental principles. Founding principles and corporate philosophies might be called a company's DNA. They are the company's mission, the ideal that it seeks to become. To reject these things is to render the company meaningless. Indeed, its very existence becomes precarious.

To constantly seek to innovate while continuing to protect the company's fundamental principles may seem difficult to accomplish, but I think it is really very simple. All you have to do is take the long view. All you have to do is pursue your work while looking a few years down the road, but without shifting your point of origin. If you ever have trouble making a decision, go back to where you started—go back to your roots.

Ideally, your starting point—that is, your management philosophy—should be shared by all employees, even as individual employees apply their own personalities to their particular jobs.

Going back to your roots is all the more important in times like these, when the economic environment is rough. I believe that by taking a close look at where you came from, while also taking the long view, you will see the way forward to a company that endures, whose employees are happy.

Afterword

Something really wonderful happened recently. By chance, I was told the same thing at two different restaurants: "We can always tell when a customer is an Ina Foods employee—their table manners, the way they clean up after themselves, and the kindness they show toward our staff are all a dead giveaway."

This made me feel very proud of our employees. They are upstanding members of society, and I respect them for it.

Being involved in corporate management has given me the opportunity to think deeply about the reasons for a company to exist and how we human beings should live our one-and-only lives. The goal of life is to be happy. The goal of a manager is to make his employees happy. What should be done to achieve these goals?

I have my own desires and dreams, of course. Sometimes I wonder what might have happened if I had moved the Ina Foods headquarters to Tokyo, right in the middle of Ginza. I am sure I would have been led astray by materialism and the desire for fame. Perhaps it is because we are surrounded by the rich, natural landscape of the Ina Valley that I came upon the notion of slow-growth tree-ring management.

Tree rings exhibit a mechanism for endurance. Trees do not stop growing even during years with bad weather. Their rings are narrower, but they continue to grow at a pace that is right for them. They do not say, "Well, the weather is bad this year, so I'm not going to grow." It is the same with our company. I want us to continue to grow steadily at our own pace, even if it is a slow one, without blaming others or our environment. This is the essence of tree-ring management.

In this book, I have talked about the nature of corporate management based on my own thinking, practice, and experience. In a world where the economy is booming and everything is running full steam ahead, perhaps no one will pay any attention. But I have aspired to tree-ring management even in good times.

I have sensed that the world has shown a growing interest in the way Ina Foods is managed, partly because we have seen an increase in people from other companies visiting our headquarters.

We have received visits, not only from representatives of small and medium-sized enterprises, but also by directors and managers from some of Japan's biggest corporations, including Toyota Group companies, Lawson, Nippon Life Insurance, Tokio Marine and Nichido Fire

Insurance, Hitachi Cable, Teijin, and Murata Manufacturing—even a visit from the president of the Japanese
branch of The Ritz-Carlton Hotel Company, known for
providing the best customer service in Japan.

I am convinced that if more companies take another
look at their own definition of how things really ought to
be and find a way to ride out these difficult times, then
surely their employees, and our society, will move in the
direction of greater happiness.

Thank you for taking the time to read this book.

Hiroshi Tsukakoshi

Hiroshi Tsukakoshi

Tsukakoshi was born in 1937 in Komagane, a small city in Nagano Prefecture, Japan. He dropped out of Ina Kita High School after contracting tuberculosis and later joined Ina Food Industry Co., Ltd. in 1958. He became President in 1983 and assumed the post of Chairman in March 2005. In recognition of his achievements in establishing a stable supply system for kanten and for pioneering new markets in areas such as health care, biotechnology, and nutritional care, Tsukakoshi was awarded the Government of Japan's Medal of Honor with Yellow Ribbon in 1996. In 2002, he received the Outstanding Businessperson Award, the highest award from Nikkan Kogyo Shimbun Company honoring outstanding managers of small and medium-sized enterprises. In 2006, as recognition for his accomplishments of achieving 48 consecutive years of rising sales and rising profits, and for his company's philosophy, track record, and future potential, Ina Food Industry Co., Ltd. received the Good Company Award Grand Prize from the Medium and Small Business Research Institute. An amateur photographer, Tsukakoshi enjoys capturing scenes of nature in his hometown area of Ina, Nagano and around the world. He is the author of *Ii kaisha o tsukurimasho* (Let's Build a Good Company) and co-author of *Kofuku e no genten kaiki* (Getting Back to the Basics of Happiness), both published by Bunya. In 2011, he received the Order of the Rising Sun, Gold Rays with Rosette from the Government of Japan.

（英文版）リストラなしの「年輪経営」
いい会社は「遠きをはかり」ゆっくり成長
Tree-Ring Management: Take the Long View and Grow Your
Business Slowly

2015年3月27日　第1刷発行

著者: 塚越 寛
訳者: ハート・ララビー
発行所: 一般財団法人 出版文化産業振興財団
〒101-0051 東京都千代田区神田神保町3-12-3
電話: 03-5211-7282（代）
ホームページ: http://www.jpic.or.jp/

印刷・製本所 大日本印刷株式会社

ISBN 978-4-916055-46-0